JANE

# The Book
## of
# Outrageous
# Prayers

BLESS YOU!

## By

## Bob W. Anderson

i

ISBN:  978-1-312-79915-8

# About the Author

Bob W. Anderson graduated from Life Pacific College with a ministerial degree and won a scholarship to California Institute of the Arts where he studied film production.

Bob was on staff at The Church On The Way in Van Nuys, California, for nine years, three of which were served on Pastoral Staff as Director of Prayer Ministries working alongside Dr. Jack Hayford and the late Dr. Scott Bauer.

He has written and co-written nine books, as well as produced, directed and written films for fifteen years, winning 49 awards and two Emmys.

## Other Books by Mr. Anderson

### *The Secret of Shar*
A romance mystery novel

### *Spike Freedom*
A superhero comic book

**God is not religious.
He's relational.**

God is not imprisoned
by any man-made box;
He is loose, armed and dangerous.

**God is good.  All the time.
In fact, He is far more "extremely good"
than most people dare to imagine.**

# INTRO

## Prayer is More Than Wishing

In the synoptic gospels of Matthew and Luke, Jesus gives us a guideline for powerful prayer that contains key essentials.

One ingredient of His instructional prayer is a very bold request: "Your Kingdom come, Your will be done on earth as it is in Heaven."

Although many of us have heard or prayed those words countless times, The Lord's Prayer contains one of the most electrifying concepts in all of Scripture — that we're given permission to call for *Heaven to invade earth.* That concept is so huge, we could easily fail to comprehend its majesty if we lose sight of God's original plan for humanity at Creation.

In Genesis 1:28, God blessed Adam and Eve by saying to them: "Be fruitful and multiply, and replenish the earth, and subdue it..."

Let's zoom to the key words of that verse:

| English | Hebrew | Meaning |
|---------|--------|---------|
| "Fruitful" | *Parah* | to increase |
| "Multiply" | *Rabah* | to have abundance, excel, be full of, become great |
| "Replenish" | *Mala* | to possess wholly, accomplish, overflow, furnish |
| "Sudue" | *Kabash* | to conquer |

What an amazing composite picture of how life *should* be! We were created by God to conquer new horizons, to fully possess our destiny, to accomplish great things, be well-equipped, to enjoy abundant overflow, and to increase.

*That* is God's desired program for the Human Race. He said so right at Creation.

So what's the problem? Why is life on Planet Earth so screwed up? The answer, of course, is the Fall of Mankind and the resulting consequences of *sin* (Genesis 3).

The account of the Fall and the ensuing story of redemption warrant another book entirely, but the essence of the matter is that God wants to permeate every level of life, fill it, and fix it because He is, by nature, a Redeemer.

Even at Creation — before the Fall — *conquering* was a big part of the adventure. Now that we're living on a broken planet, the urgency for all of us to be *overcomers* is greater than ever.

All blessings freely given to us at Creation are *now* — after the Fall — apprehended only through forceful conquest: "The Kingdom of God suffers violence and the violent *take it by force*" (Matt. 11:12).

In other words, life on earth does not automatically provide the full measure of all that was originally designed for us. On the contrary, the world is very hostile to our created purpose.

Life is war, and there are many enemies working against us. In addition to our own sinful nature, which is totally capable of destroying life on its own, dark spiritual forces seek to ruin human lives as well as entire cultures through countless strategies. And essentially, the top priority of spiritual wickedness in high places is to prevent Heaven from being established on earth through ordinary people (Eph. 6:12).

What's the solution? The abundant life of Heaven first requires our relationship with God to be restored through faith in Jesus Christ. Only *then* can we enter a partnership with the Creator to help re-establish His Kingdom on earth.

That Kingdom is not a religious realm or an endless liturgy, but rather a relational realm packed with miracles, healing, hope, power, restoration and the smashing of limitations at every level.

Man created religion, but God created the Universe and everything from strawberries to kittens, from math to snowflakes, from marital sex to laughter, from beauty to rich fulfillment.

Every good gift comes from the "Father of Lights," including dreams of the human heart. He alone knows how to put life together and expand our adventure beyond horizons we've never seen.

But as Jesus told us, it takes prayer, OUTRAGEOUS prayers that boldly believe God is good, prayers that are based on the conviction that God greatly desires to give us His Kingdom, and that He is a rewarder of those who seek Him with all of their hearts. (Luke 12:32; Heb. 11:6)

———————

———————————

PART ONE of this book presents the author's spiritual journey leading to the very moment he was suddenly consumed by "a million volts" of Perfect Love — a taste of Heaven on earth.

PART TWO escorts the reader through 52 outrageous prayers designed to connect ordinary people with life-changing Power.

PART THREE reveals the single-most profound secret that the author has discovered in more than 30 years of searching.

———————————

# Part One

## How It All Started

The first Earth-shattering event that rocked my world happened in my own backyard.

It would prove to be the first in a series of God invasions which ultimately helped bring this book into existence.

I grew up in California's San Fernando Valley. I also grew up in a spiritual vacuum. Our household didn't have any definitive faith to speak of, and my dad left the family when I was just five years old. My mom worked very hard raising my sister and me, and I think she did a stellar job. But there was still a conspicuous void, both in our household and within my little kid heart. As a result, even as a young person, the idea of God became mysteriously attractive. (My mom relayed the concept to me, but in very sketchy terms.)

Over the next few years following my parents' divorce, my wistful hopes grew that maybe the Creator would be willing to help people with their problems, even willing to help a mere kid just seven years old.

That idea prompted me to ask Him.

One summer evening, I was playing with my dog in our backyard. Everything was luminescent with the steely glow of a full moon. Soon, I began chatting with God about my young life, almost in a playful and flirtatious way, accompanied by a little dance. After all, the idea that the Maker of everything might actually be listening to me was a thrill—a direct antidote to the agony suffered from my earthly dad having left the family.

The chatty, one-way conversation ended with a direct challenge: "So, God, if You're really there, would You please talk to me right now?"

He did.

His audible voice filled the sky like thunder, and it shook the Earth as He affirmed that He was, in fact, the God of the Universe. His voice was so loud and so huge, it was like a bomb going off, and yet it was also tender. The sound emanated from everywhere. The Voice was strikingly youthful yet, at the same time, ageless. The magnitude of that Voice, speaking with absolute authority over the elements, caused me to melt.

I was terrified.

I ran into the kitchen with my heart pounding nearly out of my chest. The ambient sound of my shoes skittering across the kitchen linoleum and the crash of the wooden screen door slamming behind me were almost inaudible beneath the roar of cardiovascular throbs filling my ears.

I made it to the hallway and stuck my head into a cabinet, frantically and witlessly sorting hardware objects—for no intelligent reason other than to try and divert the Super Attention that I had just summoned from beyond the Milky Way. Deep down, I was elated; but my body and soul couldn't handle it, and I was shaken to the core.

I knew that life would never be the same.

What I *didn't* know is that the encounters with All Power coming in the years ahead would be even more stunning.

## The Journey Continues

Because of this outrageous event that I experienced with God at age seven, I had no doubts, while growing up, that He existed.

Still, throughout most of my teen years, I resisted the idea that I needed to accept Jesus Christ on His terms. I liked Him at a distance, as sort of a "cosmic friend," but I recoiled at the idea of allowing Him to become anything more.

To me, the words "Savior" and "Lord" seemed like religious and hostile words. That's primarily because throughout my childhood we had a very religious neighbor who found ways to make my life miserable. She consistently heaped guilt on me through spurious accusations based on one imagined failure after another. And she did this with such sweet, self-absorbed piety. As a result, I wanted no part of the world she represented.

When my high school years came, two friends told me about their faith in Jesus. Eventually, I relented and said the prayer that I had resisted for so many years. I asked Him to come into my life, which He did—in a huge way.

I immediately began going to every Bible study I could find, and I also attended a large church in Los Angeles. This all happened very quickly during the first few months of my new faith journey.

## God in a Box

While attending a number of classes and seminars, I soon noticed a curious thing. Among the several Bible teachers and skilled instructors I was privileged to sit under, two presented a theme that surfaced repeatedly. In essence, that theme was that God no longer does miracles or awesome things as we read about in the

Bible, especially, the spectacular things found in the Book of Acts.

These two teachers stressed that since we now have the Bible, we no longer need God to act like God in those powerful ways. Miracles were for an earlier era, they said. Consequently, everything in the Bible pertaining to power and miracles was reprocessed by these teachers through a lens that reduced the Scriptures to mere doctrines devoid of any current power.

They presented a realm of faith in which we could control and administrate everything *about* God, and to freely do so without *God Himself* inconveniently getting in our way. Of course, these teachers would have never put it in those terms, but at the end of the day, that's exactly what they were presenting to those of us sitting in their summer Bible classes.

Of course, that theological position required fancy verbal footwork as they danced around a plethora of Bible verses that proclaimed otherwise.

As a new kid of faith, I watched them dance and contort in order to avoid blatant denial of what the Bible said, while at the same time, attempting to present a sterilized, plastic replica of biblical faith that ripped power and miracles right out of everything the Scriptures actually proclaimed.

So, even as a young person new to faith, I knew something was fishy—big time. Respectable men were redefining God according to their own lackluster experiences and unbelief.

Six months prior to asking Jesus into my life, I had been drawn into Eastern mysticism. During those months, I began experiencing oppression by spiritual forces that I didn't even believe existed. Hellish stuff was beginning to crowd into my life with increasing fury.

The more I practiced transcendental meditation and studied the teachings of the mystic gurus, the worse the mental torment became. I'm not talking about depression here, I'm talking about horrific attacks that defy explanation, ghastly oppression right out of a horror movie, all driven by invisible things with personalities. I was tasting firsthand the power of spiritual darkness—the very thing I had always insisted was nothing more than superstition espoused by the uneducated. The escalating torment made me even more desperate for the truth.

I believe this melodramatic onslaught came at me as severely as it did because God had already revealed Himself to me in a spectacular way in my childhood, and now I had essentially turned my back on Him by following a religion that relegated Jesus to being only one teacher among many great teachers—not God and Savior, as Jesus Himself said He was.

We are responsible for the light we are given, and I was certainly being held accountable for the epic revelation God had graciously given me at age seven. That revelation included a thumbprint, that is, a very specific God-identity attached to it, along with a command to believe and to follow. So, when that galactic flash bulb went off in my backyard, there was a tremendous spiritual imprint instantly imparted into the film of my soul, an illuminated image that pointed right to the Person of Jesus Christ.

Because the responsibility and accountability that came with that encounter was significant, the consequences were weighty when I abandoned it all. That's why things got so bad so fast when I deliberately wandered away from the God-encounter I had been given twelve years prior. Choosing to disregard that Supreme Identity and follow a religion that taught about other gods was a betrayal, and God's mercy allowed me to see the contrast all too clearly.

The spirit of our culture embraces the virtues of an open mind, as long as the bottom line is anything but Jesus and the Bible. Ironically, that same cultural mindset violates its own edict and becomes immediately closed at the mention of the true biblical Jesus. If, with an open mind (like I had at age seven), you discover the very specific identity of the God of all creation and you embrace Him, you are then branded by our culture as having a closed mind simply because you've made a definitive decision about a definitive personal God, based on evidence you deem worthy enough for your faith. That is not a closed mind. In all fairness, I would call that a resolved and decisive mind.

### Where's the Power?

Therefore, when I became a believer in Jesus and saw the awesome power of God acted out in the Bible, I wanted to experience it firsthand. I had already suffered from "the dark side of the Force," so to speak. Where was the *True* Power?

Meanwhile, week after week, those two highly respected Bible teachers (whose names are still recognized today) kept drilling home their dogmatic position that God's miracles are no longer available and that the terms of God's power had somehow expired like a carton of milk.

Without expressing any vocal protest in their classes, I inwardly rejected their opinions—all the more determined to find an answer.

6

During the third month of my faith journey, a youth group I had joined embarked on a mission trip. We were going to share our faith at the University of California at Berkeley, right on the steps of Sproul Hall; and also at San Quentin Prison, where riots were breaking out because of an explosive and internationally watched conflict that centered around those known as The Soledad Brothers.

The idea of sharing our faith in the midst of such a violent crowd motivated us to pray for God's protection and guidance for the days ahead. As we did, I noticed my friends were gently praying in another language. The language was so elegant that it sounded like symphonic music, the way you might imagine angels would speak.

I looked up and interrupted them, "Hey! What are you guys doing?"

I hardly waited for them to answer as they started to read to me a passage from the second chapter of Acts. I said, "Listen, I want it! How do I get this?" They said they would all pray for me that night at Polly's apartment; she was one of my new friends. I was thrilled.

### Beyond Special Effects

That night, we all sat in a circle on the floor in Polly's den. My four friends were smiling with anticipation, and so was I. The God who had shaken the Earth while visiting me in my backyard when I was seven was about to visit me again! I wasn't sure what it would look like, but since I knew such encounters are in the Bible, I was convinced something wonderful was coming my way. We all closed our eyes as my friends placed their hands on me and started praying for me to be filled with the Holy Spirit.

The first thing that stunned me was that I could still see my friends . . . *after closing my eyes.* I thought to myself, "Hmm. This is interesting."

I then "looked"—with my eyes still shut—at my friend Gwennie. I could see a pinpoint of light in her right shoulder, and I was riveted. I had never experienced anything like this before—I had never seen anything with my eyes closed, let alone with special effects revealing the spiritual dimension.

Things got even more intense. The pinpoint of light was gathering volume and force. As I watched, it began traveling down Gwennie's arm. It quickly took on the characteristics of both light and water: shining, shimmering, and splashing.

With my eyes still closed, I "watched" this Light-Water also flowing down the arms of my other friends as they continued to pray for me.

Before long, the Light-Water was like a tornado swirling around me. I was absolutely overwhelmed with the sweetness and force of God's love, something I'd never experienced before. I soon realized the *what* I was watching (the Light-Water) was actually a *Who* . . . the Person of the Holy Spirit.

And then, as if all of this weren't enough, the Light-Water anthropomorphically paused and seemed to look at me, and then He shot into my chest and stomach.

### I Was Toast

At this point, there are no words to convey the experience. My best description is that it was one million volts of **perfect love**. This was *not* a religious experience. Nor was it merely a pleasant mood that settled over me by way of hypnotic suggestion or self-fulfilled yearnings. In fact, it wasn't just a feeling, though I certainly felt it! This was an experience that became a state of being, and it went far beyond, while including, my intellect.

I would never describe what happened as an alien invasion or a mystical oneness with the Universe. It wasn't a bizarre emotional trip or a hippie flashback. It was not religious ecstasy or a trance. (I use these words the way that a cynical newspaper reporter or journalist would typically spin it).

It *was*, foremost, extreme romance. There was a sudden intimacy between me and the One I had never really known, and yet He felt to me like the most passionate and intimate friend I had always known. As His love kept rushing through every cell of my being, it was extremely familiar, yet absolutely new. Gender was irrelevant; this relationship far exceeded any human limitations or definition.

I kept thinking, "*This* is what *every* human craves! Oh my gosh! Everyone wants this! *This* is what we all crave, we were made for this—the whole world!"

I was smashed by love—undone, as if the most intense lovesick crush had exploded into the greatest releasing fulfillment, flooding every inch of my being, and I was left helpless and, frankly, "ga-ga" over the One who was overwhelming me.

I was toast.

There is no love a person could desire that *wasn't* contained in the immersion of the Holy Spirit as I experienced Him. The human brain can't even assemble the concept. And what I've attempted to describe in the above paragraphs about my experience falls way short. The actual experience was ten to the hundredth power more than words can express.

Following this extraordinary experience, I remained "drunk in the Spirit" for three days (intoxication as seen in Acts 2). In fact, I could hardly speak during that time. Instead of English, the only thing I was good for was what seemed to be an angelic language—definitely not of this Earth, as far as I could tell. Even when I tried to ask my friends at dinner something mundane like, "Would you pass the salt?", there was an outpouring of Heaven-speak. All of us were in a constant state of hilarity. "Fun" is too small a word for that epic week!

There's a biblical phrase describing God as "the desire of the nations." This means God is the ultimate fulfillment of human desire—not specifically for the religious of heart—but rather for every person on Earth, whether it's a teenager on drugs, a Wall Street hedge fund manager, or a Middle Eastern terrorist . . . if you're human, *this* is the love and the Person you were made for.

Ironically, the religious of heart seems to be one of the largest categories of people on the planet who consistently tend to reject God's manifest love and power. This theatrical irony is best illustrated by the religious Pharisees of Jesus' time. The ones most zealous for God hated Him the most. That's because the realm of religion became their realm of control. And God is not controllable.

I was blessed with this amazing encounter with Him not because I'm special or because I'm somehow more worthy than anyone else, but simply because I was that hungry. Here's one reason for my hunger . . .

### The Emptiness of Happiness

Even during high school, before I gave God a formal invitation into my life, I would often cry myself to sleep at night because I was so desperate to know Him. This is not because I was religious or virtuous in any way, however. I'll explain.

The tears that came on most nights happened during the most rewarding and enjoyable years of my youth. I was not a sad person; I was actually extremely happy! I totally loved high school. I was winning oodles of national photography awards (a passion of mine), and my friends and I had a continual blast pursuing all sorts of creative adventures.

Crying myself to sleep was the residual effect from my encounter with God when I was seven. The radiation of that terrifying, backyard "nuclear blast" left a calling card, as it were, deep inside my soul. It's as if I had been left with living powder burns inside of me that never stopped burning. Even the most wonderful life couldn't compare with Him, nor could it recapture His presence.

In other words, God had me at "hello." And I simply couldn't get over Him. Even happiness couldn't replace Him. The night He spoke to me is the night He ruined me for being without Him.

### *Lunch Is Ready*

A few years later into my faith journey, my friend, Sandi and I visited an orphanage in Mexico about a half hour outside of Tijuana. It was a small place with about thirty kids. We dug ditches to help install some new pipes in the ground.

Soon, word came to us that the orphanage had run out of food. Sandi and I counted up the change we had in our pockets, and it wasn't much. Even so, we took what we had, went to the store, and at least we were able to buy two bags of groceries. I put the two bags of groceries in the trunk of my '69 Pontiac Le Mans, slammed the trunk shut, and drove off.

When we arrived at the orphanage, I opened up the trunk, and what Sandi and I saw made us both scream with near hysteria: there were FIVE bags of groceries, not the TWO that we put in there!

*God had multiplied food for the orphans right there in the trunk of my car!*

It took hours for us to begin recovering from that amazing miracle. Then again, why were we so surprised? Jesus had *already* shown us in the Gospels His ability to multiply food. And back then, it was even more amazing because Jesus had to manage it all without the assistance of a '69 Pontiac.

Over the next few decades there continued many more miracles, angelic visits, new encounters with the Holy Spirit, healings, and astounding events which led to the writing of this book.

I will resume with this story and some observations in Part Three: *A Theology of Intimacy*, which includes the most astounding spiritual discovery that I've ever learned in twenty-five years of searching. It's an ancient key that can put a spiritual nuclear reactor in your life like nothing else can!

But for now, let's proceed with the fifty-two strategic prayers.

# Part Two

## The 52 Prayers

The fifty-two prayers presented on the following pages emerged from the kind of life experiences you've just read about. It's important to note that the power of the fifty-two prayers doesn't come from any literary craftsmanship or eloquence on my part; they're actually quite simple, so that they can be prayed easily out loud. Neither does their power come by merely reading them.

Their power comes by *praying* them, and doing so with one's heart open to as much belief as possible. Don't worry about how much faith you have or don't have. It's really just an issue of maintaining a childlike heart, and applying the faith you *do* have.

And really, perhaps even more than faith, these prayers require significant courage. It won't take long for you to recognize that these are not ordinary prayers. You'll soon see that they are designed to unleash power into your life—dangerous power. I say dangerous not because it's negative or destructive but rather because the resulting power, in time, will transcend your control and go beyond anything you've ever known.

The power is also dangerous in terms of effecting change. These prayers are designed to rock your world. The most important thing to remember, however, is that the Absolute Power you'll be unleashing into your life just happens to LOVE you . . . more than you can imagine.

Finally, it's dangerous power because God will be promoted in your life above anything else, elevated to His proper place as God . . . unrestricted and perhaps just a bit wild.

For every one of the following prayers
that express your heart . . .

**Pray them out loud.**
***Really* loud.**

There are fifty-two prayers in this book.
You can read one a day and repeat them
so that you'll go through the book
seven times in one year.
Or . . .
you can park on each prayer
for the entire week
and go through all fifty-two in one year.

Also, review the Scriptural references for further study.

**PLEASE REMEMBER:**
*The awesome power of these prayers*
*is not unleashed by merely reading them . . .*
*but by <u>PRAYING</u> them!*

Do read the "Concept of the Prayer" first.

Then, approach the actual prayer
just as a ski jumper zooms down an "inrun"
toward a take-off ramp
seeking to go as far as possible.

In other words, pray the written prayer,
build momentum, and after you do,
keep the topic alive before God,
embellishing and customizing your prayer
in your own words.

# Concept of Prayer 1
*Pain From The Past*

We all have bruises and wounds from our past. But why let any of that continue a moment longer?

We can invite God into the middle of our pain. He doesn't need to be persuaded to help us. After all, God is love, and He's already given us an awesome array of promises that assure us He will restore all things that have been lost, stolen, or damaged in our lives.

Someone might say, "Well, if God is sovereign, He would have already healed me by now . . . if He *really* wanted to."

The mystery is that God, in His sovereignty, decided long ago to give us the power of prayer. Some things only happen when we pray. We're in sort of a partnership with God in this life: "God & Sons, Inc."

It's a privilege to be able to activate His promises by asking. This access is only based on relationship, and it is God's good pleasure to respond to our requests with dynamic solutions that are so astounding and far-reaching that we never could have achieved any of it ourselves.

*Jer. 33:6-8    Isa. 30:26    Isa. 51:3*
*Lk. 12:32    Jn. 8:36    1 Th. 5:17    3 Jn. 2*

# prayer 1

## *Pain From The Past*

God, I may not be aware of all the deep wounds of my own heart. So I invite You to show me places of pain from my past (but maybe not all at once!).

As You bring specific wounds before me with new clarity, would You speak Your words of healing to me that address each issue—words that will set me free?

By the power of the Holy Spirit, please clean up the debris of my past so it doesn't stay inside of me like an old bullet or a piece of rusty shrapnel from a past war . . . a barb that keeps hindering my freedom and joy.

I agree with Your Word about the crucial importance of forgiving people who have hurt me. For every painful incident that I can think of in which someone has wounded me, either intentionally or by accident, I now forgive each one *by name*. I totally release them; they owe me nothing. Please flow Your healing power to them and to me.

[Continue praying in your own words.]

# Concept of Prayer 2
## *Faceless Father*

Most of us can picture Jesus, and we can imagine the Holy Spirit . . . but the term "Heavenly Father" can cause a complex emotional reaction inside many of us. Even the simple word "dad" can trigger emotional pain from childhood. If we pray to our Father in Heaven while perceiving Him as a faceless blank—or worse— then we'll likely struggle under an *orphan spirit.*

An orphan spirit prevents us from living with a sense of family security and personal value—an inner affirmation that we all desperately need.

Even if we succeed in life with impressive accomplishments, or if we make tons of money, or if we have lots of friends, there will always remain inside of us a deep vacuum if there's any disconnect from our earthly father or from our Father in Heaven. That's because we were created for intimacy with fatherhood. It's absolutely foundational, and it's from this fountainhead that rivers of blessing, significance, and identity are designed to flow.

God's solution is to provide for us a *spirit of adoption*—the spirit of total acceptance—the gateway to intimacy with Him who is our Ultimate Dad.

*John 14:8-10  Rom. 8:15*
*1 Cor. 15:49   2 Cor. 3:18   James 4:8*

# prayer 2

*Faceless Father*


God, I'm having trouble knowing you as my "Heavenly Father." That term is not a happy thought for me.

In every place where I have resentment, rage, disappointment, or distrust regarding my earthly dad, please neutralize those negatives.

I forgive my earthly father for any pain he's caused me. I bless him. Even when he's in the grave, I'm determined to honor him.

Papa God, redefine fatherhood for me. Please create a relationship between You and me that hasn't yet existed. Please fill in the emotional blanks for me.

I need to sense how valuable I am to You. I want to hear the sound of Your laugh and how it feels to be held by You. I want to feel Your hand in mine.

Heavenly Father, burn up every obstacle that hinders me from knowing You well and replace all of my childhood pain with Your love.


[Continue praying in your own words.]

# Concept of Prayer 3
*Money!*

When you think about it, money is weird stuff. The love of it is the root of all kinds of evil, and yet it's also the very thing needed to feed orphans and build cities. We need money in daily life—we can't get away from it—and yet few of us are experts at managing it. On one hand, stress from not having enough money is a common problem, and on the other hand, way too much money can (but not always) scramble people's priorities and dilute their faith.

So how do we win with money—a thing we're forced to deal with every day? There's a tension in God's Word about wealth, and He's happy to help us find the balance.

The big issue is learning how *not* to serve money from our hearts. Interestingly, that issue of serving money can go in two different directions: we can either be obsessed with gaining riches, or we can be consumed by anxiety over the lack of money. Both situations put us in a servant's position. God delights in our prosperity, but He just wants us to rule over it—even if we gain a lot of it—so that our hearts are totally His. While our hearts seek His Kingdom first, our hands can learn how to manage and increase every dollar through wisdom. In short, we need to rule over money so that it serves us as we serve God.

*Gen. 18:17-18    Prov. 8:12-21    Prov. 10:4*
*Prov. 22:4    Matt. 6:19-34    Luke 16:13*
*3 John 2    1 Tim. 6:17*    James 1:17    Ps. 35:27

# prayer 3

*Money!*

God, please help me with the issue of money!

Forgive me for any and all irresponsibility that I've practiced regarding finances.

Send me someone who can mentor me in the ways of financial responsibility. As I listen to wise counsel, please accelerate my understanding. Help me make excellent decisions throughout my financial future. I would even ask for the character and wisdom to carry significant wealth with excellence. So Lord . . .

Deliver me from every bit of debt!

Break off from me a poverty spirit!

Send me a financial mentor!

Cause me to prosper!

Give me a generous heart!

In short, help me rule over money so *it serves me* as I serve You with a first-love passion. With that kind of heart, I believe wealth You give me will naturally pour into the lives of others, and I'll become like Abraham, a man You richly blessed so that he would become a blessing to the entire world.

[Continue praying in your own words.]

# Concept of Prayer 4
## *Bless Them Anyway*

Jesus told us that we should bless people who curse us and that we should love our enemies (even though it sure isn't human nature to do this!). If we're willing to just step in the right direction, however, His Spirit will help us live it out from the heart.

When people driving on the road suddenly cut us off and almost kill us, our response can be less than gracious. We might actually feel poison rushing to our tongues. So when people drive like that, or when it feels like people are stabbing us in the back—what if we poured out a blessing on them?

For example, if we nearly get smashed by another car, what if we were to pray a specific, forceful blessing immediately, right on the spot:

"God, give that person triple the income this year! Bless that person's family, and make them know You! Give them a fun-filled life!    And while You're at it, fulfill their dreams!"

With all of that adrenaline we'd have rushing through us at that moment—it could help energize a loud blessing with gusto, instead of yelling a curse. If we practice this, it will dramatically transform us into His image, one crazy driver at a time!

*Luke 6:45    Luke 6:28    Luke 6:35    John 7:38*

# prayer 4

## *Bless Them Anyway*

God, it's not my nature to bless those who abuse me. So I ask that You would put inside of me Your substance of character that naturally blesses everyone, good and bad, all the time.

I want this kind of response to become a reflex inside of me. I want to get to the point where I don't even think about it.

I also bring to You all of those emotional triggers inside of myself—those buttons that people push and I instantly have a horrible reaction. Could You please rewire me? I need You to reprogram me, Lord, with Your nature of love and grace.

Right now, I want to bless a number of specific people by name. I ask that you would greatly bless these people as I lift them up to you.

[Continue praying in your own words.]

# Concept of Prayer 5
## *The Designs of Wounds*

Any given wound has its own unique design and shape. Each wound also has its own story of how it came into existence, the impact and pain that caused it, how it has or hasn't healed, etc.

A wound of the heart is like any physical injury: it also has specific designs and a unique story as well.

When we think of Jesus' wounds on the Cross, the wounds that poured out blood, we know they were the gateway for our forgiveness and healing. The very designs of His suffering became the literal designs for our eternal life and restoration.

Therefore, as our Savior, Jesus is totally prepared to move His supernatural redemption through our own personal wounds, which will result in new designs of life, healing, and hope.

*Jer. 30:17   Isa. 51:3   Isa. 61:3   1 Pet. 2:24*

# prayer 5

*The Designs of Wounds*

Jesus, I lift up my wounds to You now.  Each one of them has its own design and history.

As You fill my wounds with Your healing touch, I believe that the resulting life will also have a highly unique design.  There will be an amazing story behind every wound—not just how it came to be inflicted upon me, but how you healed it, and how Your life now moves through that exact spot of former injury.

Your artistry in restoring all things is gorgeous!

God, write the story of Your restoration into my wounds, and flow Your glory out through them so I can give You credit and tell people who You really are. Make me a work of art with Your redemptive designs.

[Continue praying in your own words.]

# Concept of Prayer 6
## *Your Blood Edits My Life*

It's important to remember that when we confess our sins, Jesus' amazing blood washes them all away *completely*. When we experience His forgiveness, we're totally justified before God. As someone once said, it's "just-as-if-I'd" never sinned.

When Jesus died on the Cross with our sins, it wasn't merely a demonstration to show us that our sins are bad. He literally BECAME our sins on the Cross. Then, with those sins infused into His very being, He died, rising on the third day.

So, the totally extreme nature of the salvation Jesus gives us means that I, for example, am a dead man. Now when any accuser, like a cop with a warrant for my arrest, comes around looking to condemn me for sins of decades ago or sins of minutes ago, I've got a way out. When guilt bangs at my door, I can now say:

"Oh, are you looking for that horrible person who sinned? Well, that person is actually dead. You can't judge him or send him to prison. Yes, that's right. You won't even find him anywhere in this house or on the planet. He's gone. Dead."

*2 Cor. 5:17   1 John 1:9   Gal. 2:20   Rom. 8:1*
*Micah 7:18-19   Ps. 103:11-12   Heb. 4:14-16*
*Heb. 10:17   Isa. 1:18; 44:22*

# prayer 6

*Your Blood Edits My Life*

Jesus, because I've put my faith in You as my Savior, I'm now a dead person (since I died with You!). And the specific sins that I haven't yet confessed to You are what I bring to You now.

[Continue praying in your own words.]

Now that my sins are confessed, You've wiped them out completely. The spiritual accuser is defeated and silenced. I'm a totally *new creature*, born of Your perfect seed, and there is no condemnation against me!

God, I have no desire to be glib about sin, but Your forgiveness empowers me with complete confidence before You. Thank you, Lord!

# Concept of Prayer 7
## *Do Stuff!*

Everything Jesus does and says in the Bible tends to demand a decision from us. He continually provokes a response from us: do we love Him or hate Him? Do we believe Him or not believe Him?

We clearly see God's amazing works in the Bible, and yet Jesus had the stunning boldness to promise that all of us can do the very same miracles He did (and even greater works) by His Spirit!

Decision time . . . do we believe Him or not believe Him? Deal or no deal? Do we spin His words into mythical and vague concepts so that we can justify our unbelief and low expectations? Or do we take Him at His word as if He really means what He says? Reports of people being raised from the dead by prayers of faith are rapidly increasing. It's not just happening in Africa but also here in the States. Jesus is actually restoring missing body parts, tumors are instantly disappearing, and broken bones are getting healed on the spot.

Feeling bad about our own limited faith isn't the point (we've all struggled with unbelief). But we *can* decide to focus on the awesome possibilities of Heaven invading Earth—something God desperately wants to give us. And it all starts by simply asking.

*Matt. 10:8      Luke 1:37      Luke 7:22*

# prayer 7
## *Do stuff!*

Lord, I'm asking that You'd show up and do outrageous things. I'm talking about the stuff that's in the Bible. I'd love to pray for people who are sick, and then watch You instantly heal them—even from things that we think are tough cases, like cancer, or people mangled in car crashes. I have the audacity to ask this because *nothing* is impossible for You!

I admit, this whole topic can be a little intimidating. What if only *some* of the people I pray for get healed? Then again, taking that risk is certainly worth it for the sake of those who *do* get healed! My job is to risk asking You to do great things, while Your job is to be the All Powerful One.

Religion-as-usual is not my passion, God—*You* are! Please come down here and rip the place up with Your power so that people get healed, their lives get transformed, and in the process, we all fall madly in love with You more than ever before!

[Continue praying in your own words.]

# Concept of Prayer 8
*Invade The Pizza*


There's a difference between an objective theological precept (as wonderful as they are) and God actually showing up.

Even Forrest Gump, in the movie of the same name, discerned God's Presence, in a sense. Forrest and Lieutenant Dan had failed miserably while trying to catch shrimp on their newly acquired boat. At an important dramatic moment, Forrest said, " . . . and then . . . God showed up!"

A hurricane struck. At first, Lieutenant Dan had some rather tart words for God about the storm. Yet ultimately, God's hand moved redemptively for the two novice fishermen. In fact, it was this very storm that launched their business toward great wealth.

It's a fictional story, of course, but one in which the main character, (not even the sharpest knife in the drawer), recognized that when God "shows up", His awesome power shakes everything.


*Ex. 33:19     1 Kings 8:10-13*
*Acts 2:15-18     Eph. 5:18*

# prayer 8

## *Invade the Pizza*

Lord, would You fill our house with Your electrifying Presence? I'm not talking about something theoretical. I want You to *really* fill our house with a thick cloud of Your power and intimacy.

I'm serious, God. You and all the angels are welcome in my house. Please come here!

Even if it's pizza night or people are here to watch a football game on TV—when guests walk through the door, I'm asking that Your Presence would knock them over! I ask that we'd all get outright *drunk* in Your Spirit just like they did in Acts 2. Send angels here so that miracles happen. Do whatever You want. And let prophetic revelations flow like a river.

Instead of everyone jumping and cheering because there's a touchdown on TV, I pray that—in this house— there would be explosive celebrations because of miracles, healings, and amazing stuff!

Please, live here with us in spectacular ways so that awesome blessings constantly happen.

[Continue praying in your own words.]

# Concept of Prayer 9
*When I . . . Then You*

Whatever negatives we bring to God, He can turn those into "positives" through His Cross—the ultimate plus sign.

Whatever positives we bring to God, He is able to multiply by the "X" of His Cross, the source of endless blessing and resurrection power.

*Ps. 59:17   Ps. 103:1-5   Ps. 56:8   Rom. 12:1*

# prayer 9

## *When I . . . Then You*

When I fall apart, You rebuild me.

When I shake in fear, Your chest is at my back.

When I cry, You count my tears.

When I serve, You honor me.

When I give, You pour back many times over.

When I die to selfishness, You make me live fully.

When I sacrifice, You reward me.

When I risk in Your name, I win.

When I humble myself, You make me huge.

When I call, You answer.

When I believe, You work miracles.

In light of all this, Lord, take everything that I am and continually engineer Your way in my life.

[Continue praying in your own words.]

# Concept of Prayer 10
*No Crumbs*

Decisions over details can affect a destiny.

Because small things can have tremendous significance, especially over time, God will give us wisdom for managing all the details of life—if we ask Him.

God knows how to help us finish well in the small, day-to-day stuff, and He can effectively guide us to finish well regarding our entire lifetime.

*Heb. 12:1    1 Cor. 9:24    Acts 20:24*

# prayer 10

## *No Crumbs*

Lord, help me always finish well—in every conceivable category of life and work. I don't want to leave anything unfinished or halfway done. I don't want to leave crumbs.

If I can't stop a relationship from closing down, I want to leave things with a clean touch of responsibility, grace, generosity, forgiveness, and blessing.

If I'm finishing a project for hire, I want to do it as if I were doing it for You, completing it with polish and craftsmanship. I want to deliver to my boss or client far more than they ever expected.

I want to finish my entire life well, with character and faithfulness. I don't want to leave any messes behind me, especially as it pertains to relationships.

[Continue praying in your own words.]

# Concept of Prayer 11
*Gossip*

When someone starts to gossip about another person by tearing them down, spreading rumors, or revealing secrets, it can give us a really sick feeling. And the one thing that we may especially hate about it is . . . we may actually *enjoy* it. Something warped in the human soul tends to find gossip to be like a tasty dessert. It can almost be like a drug.

"Yeah? And then what happened? What'd they say? Can you believe it?"

Sometimes we can even get caught up like sharks in a feeding frenzy—especially when someone we don't get along with is being trashed. In a totally perverted way, gossip can make us feel better about ourselves. But gossip is listed in Proverbs as one of the seven things God hates more than anything.

*Prov. 6:16-19  Prov. 18:21  Prov. 26:22*
*Col. 4:6  Col. 3:14  2 Cor. 12:20*

# prayer 11
## *Gossip*

Lord, since gossip is a big deal to You, it needs to be an urgent issue for me. So when I'm with people and they start to tear someone down, I pray that You'd give me wisdom and sensitivity to turn those conversations around to another topic. I'd love to gently take charge in a way that nobody even realizes what I'm doing. Give me that skill.

Teach me how to weave into the conversation great qualities about the person everyone's trashing. Give me wisdom for ways to do this with grace. Make me an artist at it.

Please cause me to be a person who always builds up other people and never trash-talks anyone, even if they *are* responsible for all kinds of bad stuff.

[Continue praying in your own words.]

# Concept of Prayer 12
## *Who's Asking Anymore?*

If God never showed up again in any church, could the congregations of America keep doing business as usual, without even a hiccup?   In other words, would anyone notice if God's tangible presence never again appeared in the church sanctuary?

If God *didn't* work miracles, if He *didn't* heal people's diseases instantly, and if He *didn't* flow with prophetic revelation, would most churches even notice? Or would they get worried and ask, "Hey!  Where is the Lord?"

In the second chapter of Jeremiah, God was telling His prophet, almost with a sad voice it seemed, that the spiritual leaders and elders of Israel didn't even care enough about Him to be asking the question, "Where is the Lord?"   They were all so busy doing their religious duties that nobody cared if God actually moved in power among them or paid them a visit.

*Jer. 2:4-8     Acts 7:51*

# prayer 12

## *Who's Asking Anymore?*

Lord, please don't let me become complacent. Don't allow me to keep doing good works and religious stuff without any regard for where You are, what You're saying, or what You're doing. With my eyes riveted on You, I only want to be doing what I see *You* doing.

God, deliver me from the barrenness of a busy life. Deliver me from a blur of constant activity that has nothing to do with what You are actually doing or saying.

I don't want to *feel* that I'm being effective just because of spectacular dust in my wake. Deliver me from the illusion of success. I want my life to be like rich, black fertile soil that nourishes Your seeds; I don't want my life to be mere dust in the wind.

So God, what are You saying and doing NOW?

Show me!

[Continue praying in your own words.]

# Concept of Prayer 13
*Seven Mountains*

Many of us tend to feel helpless about making a significant difference in the world. But when we discover God's destiny for us, and we effectively invade the realm of influence that we were born to conquer, that's when amazing and wonderful things happen!

When ordinary people begin to live out their personalized destiny, they become like God-fashioned keys perfectly designed for stubborn locks that have hindered humanity or the culture for ages.

Any of us can become profound solutions to tough problems when we discover God's call on our lives.

*Deut. 28:13    Deut. 33:29    Matt. 6:10    Eph. 1:18*

# prayer 13

*Seven Mountains*

Lord, please show me Your specific call on my life.  Over which of these mountains have You selected for me to gain wisdom, expertise, and influence?

Spirituality and Church

Family

Education

Government and Law

Media and Communication

Arts and Entertainment

Business and Finance

God, please clarify and affirm the dreams that You've built into my life.  Reveal to me what my destiny is all about.  Show me how I can help bring Heaven into one or more of these seven realms of influence.

It's a big prayer, but You're a big God.

[Continue praying in your own words.]

# Concept of Prayer 14
*Prophetic Stream*

God knows exactly what each person needs to hear at any given moment—not just encouraging words, but "laser beam" words packed with insight beyond mere human knowledge, words that are literally from Heaven.

If people receive even the simplest word from the Holy Spirit through us, incredible power is unleashed so that the shattered pieces of their lives start falling into place.

Our part in the process is boldness to step out and start speaking to people the simple things God gives us … the little pictures or phrases that suddenly appear in our spirit as a result of our having asked the Lord for new prophetic insights to give away.

None of us are going to be great at this in the beginning. But it will touch God's heart to see us acting in faith and stretching ourselves as conduits of Heaven to Earth. He will meet us where we are; He will honor our faith. And if we give to people the simple words or pictures God initially gives us for them, more will quickly follow. (You've just *got* to experience this!)

Before long, the Lord will help us nail every prophetic word with amazing accuracy. The apostle Paul said we should *all* greatly desire this, because it's for *everyone*!

*Joel 2:28-29    1 Cor. 12:8-10*
*1 Cor. 14:24-25    1 Cor. 14:39*

# prayer 14

## *Prophetic Stream*

Lord, it would be so cool to get pictures and impressions from the Holy Spirit!

Would You please give me the super power of receiving Your personalized revelations for people? I promise not to sound austere or religious!

I certainly don't want to be a fortune teller (which is a totally different spirit than the Holy Spirit). But I do want to be an effective pipeline between You and other people, operating in Your supernatural power.

Make me totally *natural* (genuinely myself), while flowing with the *super* (Heaven's power).

Everyone hungers for this; everyone is desperate to break out of life as usual. And everyone wants to get in touch with power greater than themselves. Help me become an effective extension of Your life; help me deliver Your intimate messages to the world around me.

[Continue praying in your own words.]

# Concept of Prayer 15
## *Heaving*

The Jews had a Heave Offering as part of their worship ritual. Scripture doesn't say a great deal about this offering, but the breast and thigh of a ram was waved before God.

There are times of such stress in our lives that we might not have eloquent prayers to say, so all we can really do is just lift up our hearts before God and pour out our pain.

King David would often pour out his agony of soul to God without any hesitation. He felt safe being totally honest before the Lord.

*Ps. 25:1-2    Ps. 51:5-10    Ps. 62:8*
*Matt. 27:46    1 John 1:9*

# prayer 15

*Heaving*

God, it seems like everything's turned against me!

I don't even feel like You're with me! Where'd You go? Everything's falling apart! I'm insane with pain! I have so many emotions raging inside of me right now and none of them are good. I don't feel clean, I don't feel saved . . . I feel about as spiritual as sewer water!

I'm not going to accuse You of doing anything wrong. I know You're good, even when things are really bad. It just doesn't *feel* like You're good sometimes. So, I've got to do something about the boiling lava inside of my guts, or I'm going to explode.

I need to heave before You by pouring out my anxiety. It's vile stuff, God, but I've got to be honest as I lift my soul up to You, just like David did in the Psalms. I'm not hurling any of this into Your precious Face; I'm not heaving abusive speech or disrespect at You, God, but I *am* going to toss all of my honest pain into the arms of the One who died for the very stuff I'm heaving. You're the Redeemer, and I need You to redeem me from this toxic waste. You already know it's there, anyway.

Wash me. Hose me down. Give me joy again. Help me see things clearly so I can respond the right way. I want to be close to You again!

[Continue praying in your own words.]

# Concept of Prayer 16
## *A Huge Power Surge*

God seems to really enjoy taking average people and empowering them so that amazing things, like miracles, flow through their lives.

The way that God moves with awesome power among ordinary people is by His Spirit. The Bible's symbol of the Holy Spirit is oil. The Bible's term "anointed" means to be smeared with oil, which is literally to be smeared with God's Spirit.

It's very encouraging to realize that even Jesus didn't do miracles by His own power, that is, by His being God. When He became a man, He totally emptied Himself of His God powers on purpose, and then totally relied on the Holy Spirit. That way, He showed us that we, too, can do the same exact miracles He did—and even greater—because we rely on the Holy Spirit just as He did.

*Zech. 4:6    John 14:12    1 John 2:27*
*Phil. 2:5-7    Luke 4:14*

# prayer 16

*A Huge Power Surge*

God, I pray that Your power would come all over me in the highest voltage possible. I don't deserve it, but because my sins are forgiven by Jesus, I can now receive Your precious Spirit in full measure.

So my request today is simple: give me tons of power-flow by Your Spirit! Smear Your Spirit all over me! Teach me how to cooperate with that anointing, show me how to move in it, how to protect it, and how to keep getting more of it. As I get more from You, show me how to impart it to other people.

[Continue praying in your own words.]

# Concept of Prayer 17
## *Download Enchiladas*

God promises us that we can do all things through Him. He even promises us the very mind of Christ. On top of that, He has paved the way for us to constantly enjoy all kinds of revelation by His Spirit—wisdom and knowledge that come to us supernaturally.

It would be sort of silly to think that God promises us such supernatural wisdom only for religious purposes while, by contrast, we're left to fight for ourselves in our own limited strength in all of the other areas of our lives such as work, finances, relationships, family, pursuing our dreams, etc.

The power of God's Kingdom is supposed to flood everywhere, because His Kingdom has no end—not only in terms of duration, but also in terms of expanse and dimension.

In the same way that we download huge files from the internet, we need God to instantly pour into us spiritual megabytes of living knowledge and wisdom that are pregnant with solutions. We need more than just good ideas, we need the whole enchilada—the complete solution to the problem, instantly zapped down into us. We need full illumination by His Spirit at home, work, vacation, everywhere.

*1 Cor. 2:16    1 Cor. 12:8    Eph. 1:17-18*
*Acts 2:28    Phil. 4:13    Luke 1:33*

# prayer 17

## *Download Enchiladas*

Lord, please give me downloads by Your Spirit. I really need complete solutions for incredibly challenging problems.

I also need You to fill me with so much wisdom and knowledge that I can pursue dreams You've given me. I need strategies of the Spirit, insights geared to my conquering new territory.

I pray this downloading of Your wisdom wouldn't just be a one-time thing. I ask that it would become a way of life—even for my career. I'd love to constantly be walking out what You give me from these downloads.

It would even be fun if You'd give me an invention, a book, or something way "outside the box" that would become an industry-changer or a breakthrough that rocks the world.

Such a thing would really bring credit to You and Your creative power, because every time it happened, I'd sure know it wasn't me!

[Continue praying in your own words.]

# Concept of Prayer 18
## *Your Breath*

So what is it, exactly, that we want from our spiritual journey? What is it that most captures our hearts?

Does the Scripture say, "Taste and see that *serving the Lord* is good?" Or does it say that "tasting" involves the actual flavor of God Himself?

To taste food, we have to get intimate with it. It has to saturate our taste buds.

Soaking ourselves in God's presence is the very blow-out experience that can ignite someone to say: "Man! You guys have just *got* to taste God! Getting this close to Him is over the top!"

(Has it been a while since you felt this way?)

The kind of wild enthusiasm stated above certainly isn't religious talk. Such explosive passion comes only from actually tasting God.

In fact, if you can handle this outrageous analogy, the only way I can actually taste my wife is from a very deep kiss.

*Gen. 2:7     Ps. 17:15     Ps. 34:8*
*John 15:5     2 Cor. 2:14-16*

# prayer 18

## *Your Breath*

God, I want the fragrance of Heaven all over me because I've been with You, cheek to cheek. I want to carry the very atmosphere of Heaven with me wherever I go. When I walk into a room, I want the spiritual climate to instantly shift because You spill out through me.

Please help me soak in Your presence often. Give me a strategy to make this happen and cause my hunger for You to be like a hot furnace.

I need the best time and place to be alone with You so that it consistently becomes the center of my day and, really, the center of my life.

When we're alone together, I want You to whisper to me—I want to hear what's in Your heart. In fact, I want Your heartbeat to pound inside of me, and I want your breath to become mine.

If amazing fireworks don't instantly happen the first times I try this, I'm not giving up. I'm seeking intimacy with You for the long haul, even for the rest of my life.

[Continue praying in your own words.]

# Concept of Prayer 19
## *Our Secret Garden*

God said in His Word that the way He feels about His people is the same way a guy feels about his new bride. Wow, what an analogy!

Obviously, any groom strongly anticipates the intimacy he's going to enjoy with his new wife, and how the two of them are going to "burn the paint off the ceiling" that night!

This idea likely requires an adjustment in our thinking. Gender is irrelevant regarding how God and we relate since He is neither male nor female. All we know is, He said His love for us is just like that of a groom on a honeymoon. This means HE actually craves to be in OUR presence!

*Ps. 36:7    Isa. 62:5    Song 1:2    Song 5:1*

54

# prayer 19

## *Our Secret Garden*

I'm going to try and push aside any embarrassment I feel over this topic, God.

Teach me to fully receive Your passion for me. Cause me to be helplessly swept away in Your love. I'm not interested in a religious experience.

I want to be thrilled by Your kisses. I want to drink deeply of Your intimate tenderness. I want You to consume me and to burn my socks off with Your love. This is the very thing You've longed for with Your people throughout all of history.

I'm totally available! Take me to the stratosphere with You so that nothing else on Earth matters. I want to be alone with You. I don't care if anybody else understands this or not. This is between You and me, and we're going to have our own secret garden together.

[Continue praying in your own words.]

# Concept of Prayer 20
## *The Best Possible Outcome*

As people of faith, we can easily become dull to spiritual truth. Even important theological ideas can begin to lose their edge because we've heard them so many times.

So let's spice things up a bit with some new words. Let's ask God for:

—His best **trajectory**,

—His strategic **apogee** and **perigee**, and

—His most amazing **synchronicity** in our lives!

The translation is: let's ask God to help us be in the right place at the right time according to His timing and master plan, and to enjoy the best possible outcome for each day. In addition, we really need God to plot the course of our entire lives just as mission control would intricately plan an astronaut's journey.

While we're living our lives this way—amazing moment by amazing moment (even while taking care of the mundane business of daily life)—we can experience an awesome overlay of Heaven so that all God wants to accomplish throughout the story of our lives gets lived out.

*Prov. 16:9    Prov. 20:24    Ps. 138:8    Ps. 139:16*

# prayer 20

## *The Best Possible Outcome*

Lord, I'm not asking to become Your robot. But without my having to think about it, I want You to guide my every step. As I plan my way, I want You to plan beyond and through my plans, making everything work together amazingly well.

I want to keep running smack into miracle after miracle that You've provided for me. I want to encounter more and more spontaneous so-called chance meetings with people appointed by You—encounters that lead to great things.

I give you complete control of my schedule because I believe that You've been planning my life billions of years before I was born. You are before time, after time, and throughout all of time . . . all at once.

As a way of life, I want to continually enter doorways of astounding opportunity so I can experience awesome things that I never could have planned for myself.

Direct my feet, my conversations, my inspirations, my inventions, my calendar, and my decisions in Your awesome way!

[Continue praying in your own words.]

# Concept of Prayer 21
## Dream Detective

We're so easily consumed with our own stuff, aren't we?

For example, if we go to a party, we may obsess on whether we're dressed up enough or if we'll find our friends so that we won't feel alone.

But how cool would it be if God gives us hearts that are preoccupied with the destiny and dreams of others?

If we have a growing passion to discover what's foremost on other people's hearts, and we have a strong growing interest in the dreams that people have for their futures, it can be a very fulfilling way to navigate a party, let alone live a life.

*Phil. 2:3-4   James 5:16   Eph. 2:19-22*

# prayer 21

*Dream Detective*

Lord, create in me a heart that totally enjoys people—a heart that is fully engaged by the things that matter to them.

God, I pray that You'd help me care about other people's dreams. I would love for other people's passions to capture my heart.

I'd love to have Your insight and inspiration to help my friends become successful, and to be all that they can be.

With that kind of compassion, life could become more fun than ever!

[Continue praying in your own words.]

# Concept of Prayer 22
## *Ship At Sea*

A truly spiritual person is not an individual who has it all together. Nobody does. Everyone has faults, weaknesses, and profound frailties. We are all made of the same clay.

Great spirituality is found in people who know how to be honest about their weaknesses and who desperately seek God to fill their personal wasteland with His grace and strength.

*Isa. 40:31   Isa. 54:11-12   2 Cor. 12:10*
*Isa. 61:4-7   Ps. 27:5*

# prayer 22

## *Ship at Sea*

Lord, I feel like a ship at sea that has a broken rudder and torn sails. My hull has been battered to pieces. I'm full of discouragement, and I'm nearly fainting from the weariness of past storms. Sometimes I feel like I can't even raise up one more sail to catch Your wind.

Can You just blow on the condition of my weakness? Can You take charge of my life so I end up right over sunken treasure and amazing discoveries—riches of the deep that I never would have encountered in my own strength?

Just move me where I need to be. Capture my heart with Your breath. Speak to me. Hold me. Overflow me with Your life, God.

When I'm weak, then You're strong!

I believe that because You are so redemptive and compassionate, You can turn my sadness into dancing, my ashes into beauty, my lost state into sudden discovery, my poverty into wealth, and my emptiness into fulfillment.

[Continue praying in your own words.]

# Concept of Prayer 23
## *Self-Sabotage*

There's a strange hang-up that afflicts more people than one might expect. At the root of the problem is a deep sense of unworthiness. The quirky fruit that often emerges from that root is self-sabotage. Whether it's carried out consciously or unconsciously, the results are equally devastating.

A friend of mine counseled one young woman who had everything going for her. She had been one of the most popular girls in school as a star cheerleader and had a 4.0 grade point average, with a bright future ahead of her. But as years passed, she continually picked boyfriends who were always the same kind of guy: alcoholics who physically abused her.

Her mother came to my friend in tears, totally bewildered and shredded by her daughter's self-destructive trend. As my friend learned more about the girl, he realized that this impressive young woman saw herself as a zero, even though everyone else could plainly see that she was in every category a "ten."

The young woman's self-perception was what ruled the day, and so she continually chose men who she felt a zero deserved.

*Ps. 35:27     John 8:36*

# prayer 23
*Self-Sabotage*

God, this is a strange one. I've got some sort of mechanism in me that wants to sabotage good stuff in my life. What the heck is that? I may not even be fully aware of the extent of this quirk. Maybe I have a warped definition of humility, confusing it with self-destruction or self-defeat.

Show me, Lord, specifically where this root came from. What was it in my childhood that gave place to this thing? Throw Your light on the events that caused this.

I want to stop resisting Your blessings and Your love for me. Put Your hand on this weird mechanism of self-opposition, and replace my old, rusty engine parts with things of Your awesome engineering. I need to become like a new Mercedes on the inside, with every part of my soul working in harmonious precision.

Create inside of me a new core value, a strong sense of worth born out of Your delight over me.

Thank You, Lord, that You rejoice in my prosperity—both inside and out. And because You want to bless me, then I certainly need to feel free to receive all blessings from Your hand! Nudge me, Holy Spirit, whenever I'm tempted to forget how loved I am.

[Continue praying in your own words.]

# Concept of Prayer 24
## *Sleeping Under The Canopy*

When God promises us fabulous things in His Word, we have a decision to make regarding how we'll respond. Do we stay passive, or do we become aggressive about His promises, asking Him day and night to fulfill them?

God is pleased when people hunger and thirst after Him and the things of His Kingdom. For example, He gives all of us the promise that in the latter days He will pour out His Spirit on all mankind so that sons and daughters would prophesy, old men would dream dreams, and young men would see visions.

Are we interested in asking Him to fulfill that specific promise in us, so that we would dream His dreams, see His visions, and prophesy His words?

Or do we even give a rip?

He's waiting for our hungry response!

*Prov. 3:24    Joel 2:28    Ps. 91:4    Song 2:4*
*Isa. 4:5    Matt. 5:6    Luke 11:9    Acts 18:9*

# prayer 24

## *Sleeping Under the Canopy*

Lord, would You start visiting me in the night while I'm sleeping? I'd love to start having dreams that are from You. I'm not exactly sure what that looks like, but whatever You have for me in terms of Heaven-born dreams—I'll take them!

I'd love to have dreams that reveal stuff You're going to be doing in my life and in my friends' lives. I'd love to have angels hover over my bed and bring the atmosphere of Heaven over me like a canopy.

Help me worship You in my sleep so that Heaven spills over into the following day.

[Continue praying in your own words.]

# Concept of Prayer 25
## *Agreeable*

It seems like the entire fall of mankind in the Garden of Eden all came down to an issue of agreement. The big test for Adam and Eve was whether they were going to agree with God, or if they were going to agree with the liar snake—the mouthpiece for dark spiritual forces.

Adam and Eve's decision to believe a lie had devastating consequences—that's why pain and death are shrouding our cracked planet.

The same decision made in the Garden of Eden still plays out in our daily lives. We have an ongoing need to decide if we are agreeing with God and His Word, or if we are agreeing with the lies of spiritual darkness. The consequences are gigantic. Even subtle lies are devastating if we believe them.

*Gen. 3:13   Gen. 15:1-6   Matt. 18:19*
*John 10:27   1 John 5:10*

# prayer 25

## *Agreeable*

Lord, I need You to keep showing me where I'm disagreeing with Your truth and where I'm agreeing with lies. Throw your searchlight on lies of all kinds that have been planted into my mind and heart—even as basic as thinking You don't love me

Show me the lies that have come from events of the past, from deceiving spirits, from things people have told me, from our culture, and even from my own thoughts and doubts.

Illuminate each lie and lead me into total freedom from the power of each one. Accelerate my understanding of how You see me, and blast apart the lies with holy dynamite! I want Your truth, Jesus, to totally set me free.

Also, plant within me an internal warning system by Your Spirit so that I recognize lies as soon as they come to my ears.

[Continue praying in your own words.]

# Concept of Prayer 26
## *Make It a Reflex*

Sin kills, and it starts destroying good things inside of us really fast. If we let our hearts play with sin, even for seconds, it's like flies laying eggs in rotten meat. In no time those hideous maggots are born, and they start working their nightmarish destruction—inside of *us*!

We need hearts tuned in to God so that as soon as temptation enters the scene or as soon as we start choosing to disobey Him, the stopwatch starts ticking. Within seconds—no—within *tenths* of a second, we're whip-lashing our hearts right back to His feet, saying, "No!" to sin and "Yes!" to Jesus. This is not a legalistic stance at all. Rather, it's wisdom expressed through discipline. Grace is big enough for us when we fail; sin is devastating enough for us to run from it...*fast!*

Let's use lust as an example. When someone of the opposite sex walks through the door, a real stunning hottie who totally knocks us out—God's grace can help us glance away immediately, instead of studying his or her body and having sexual fantasies.

Willpower is a start, but we also need God to replace lust with something substantial and more powerful—His genuine *love* for people. We need hearts that view everyone as a precious individual. If we allow God to love and honor people through us—lust won't even have a chance, because love conquers all.

*Rom. 6:16   Prov. 20:9   Jer. 15:19*
*Isa. 1:18   Isa. 61:10   1 Pet. 4:8*

# prayer 26

## *Make It a Reflex*

Lord, I don't want to fight temptation. Instead, I don't even want to step into the boxing ring.

Give me a new experience of Your holiness—that thrilling sense of wholeness which is being genuinely myself in Jesus. The more I just walk in Your Spirit, sin loses its grip on me and I avoid sin's destructive force that wants to shred who I am in You.

But I need Your help. Teach me how to choose goodness and obedience as a reflex. Fill me with the pleasure of choosing good over wrong.

Most of all, I continue to ask for love: love for You, love for Your Word, love for people. With my heart bathed in that, sin will implode and blow away.

[Continue praying in your own words.]

# Concept of Prayer 27
## *Sexual Freedom*

God designed sex to be stellar, explosive, and amazing . . . but only inside the boundaries of marriage. His Word is clear that sex is only for a husband and wife—and that's it.

Sex is so intimate, it's no wonder that God commands that it should only happen between the two people He has joined together as one flesh.

So if we've ever had sexual encounters with someone we weren't married to, we need God to cut that connection by spiritual surgery. We had no legal grounds for being force-joined together through sex. Now we need to break each soul-tie—that residual liability that hangs over us like a debilitating weight, still hindering the purity of intimacy He has designed for us to enjoy.

*1 Cor. 6:16     1 John 1:9*

# prayer 27

## *Sexual Freedom*

God, You know the sexual stuff I've fallen into at various times in my life. I've transgressed the boundaries You set in your Word, and You know exactly what I'm talking about—You were there when I did it!

I know You forgive me for all of my sins, and I'm not here to beat myself up. But, I do need to do some homework.

I'm going to write on a piece of paper the names of everyone I've had sex with. I'm going to destroy that paper, but before I do, I'm going to specifically repent for my part in the sin, and pray for each one of those people. I'm going to pray for Your blessing and forgiveness for each one. Then, I'm also going to ask You, name by name, to break the spiritual soul-connections that were created between me and each one of those people that I became sexually intimate with. God, Your power is making this happen—it's not just a psychological exercise!

I'm also going to pray for breakthroughs in my life so that the richest possible sexual experience in marriage would come by Your power. Teach me to be a lover after Your own design, and make all things totally new again.

[Continue praying in your own words.]

# Concept of Prayer 28
*A Sliver in My Heart*

It happens to all of us. Someone offends us just a tiny bit, and a very small sliver of unforgiveness forms in our hearts. It's almost unperceivable, so we let it stay there.

That sliver doesn't seem like a big deal. But have you ever noticed what happens? When we're in the room with that person, we avoid eye contact. Oh, sure, if we're forced into it, we can glance at their face with a smiling "Hello!" and move on. But ...we move on.

That's not a good place to be.

Even the tiniest sliver can get infected and spread its poison.

We need God to show us how to make things right with others. Slivers in the heart are perfect opportunities to blend the spiritual and the practical. After we forgive such people in prayer, we should put feet to it. Maybe if we just buy them a latte—half-caf, whipped—(just as they like it), maybe that will get things rolling again in our hearts and in our relationship with them.

*Matt. 5:23-24    Luke 6:41    Rom. 12:18*

# prayer 28

## *A Sliver in My Heart*

Lord, the hurt I feel from this one person whose name I lift up to you now is just a small sliver in my heart. It doesn't seem like a big deal. Even so, I forgive them right now, by name. And I pray for a blessing on them. Please heal our relationship.

Though I forgive them, I probably need to mend things with them in a practical way as well, even if they know nothing about my little sliver.

Show me the best way to do this.

[Continue praying in your own words.]

# Concept of Prayer 29
## *Family Tree*

We all receive blessings from our ancestors and through our parents—good things, whether talents, special gifts, or a tangible inheritance.

But in every family, there's also a sin-infected root system—no matter how large or small—that's not of God's design. It's a network of strange weaknesses, patterns of sin, and pockets of dysfunction that have emerged over time, compounded by a multitude of factors. It's like an ungodly inheritance.

Most of us can detect, over the years, these dark themes laced throughout our families. They may not seem to be openly sinister, but even when these shadows are subtle, they are enough to shackle us from being everything we were meant to be.

That's because humanity, at best, is frail, and spiritual forces that hate us want to take advantage of those negative family traits, leverage them against us, keeping the toxic roots growing. That's why it takes bold action on our part to uproot every one of them as God shows us what they are.

*Rom. 3:10    2 Kings 15:9    Neh. 9:2*

# prayer *29*

## *Family Tree*

Lord, I pray that You would kill the infected root of my family tree—not the good stuff, but the threads of bondage, hidden shadows, and ropes that want to control me like a puppet or hold me back from my destiny.

Show me the specific areas that I need to saturate in prayer so that my family and I can be totally free.

All of the curses spoken against my ancestors, the sins of my fathers as well as my own failures—I bring them all under the blood of Jesus. Kill and reverse all of these hideous forces, God. I cancel out all of the spiritual stuff that's been given legal permission to move into my life and into my family. I ask that You only, Jesus, would be our Lord—the leader in charge of our lives.

Set my family free, so that every day is an awesome adventure of discovering life in a totally new way. Pour Your Holy water on all that you designed to flourish within the root system of our family tree.

[Continue praying in your own words.]

# Concept of Prayer 30
*Seducing Spirits*


God's Word says that there are seducing spirits who whisper lies to us. And the clay material of our hearts can so easily be hooked by subtle lies.

Seducing spirits use any number of tactics. They would even try to make us view God as undesirable. Sometimes voiceless and invisible spirits try to lie to our hearts about God, giving us bizarre flashes that try to turn us away from Him and toward evil. The spirits try to paint the face of evil as being beautiful, fun, intelligent, exciting, and cool. At the same time, those same spirits try to paint God's face with a false image that's boring, religious, or hateful.

What lies! The very spirits that want to shift our affections away from God are the same entities that want all of humanity destroyed! Jesus, on the other hand, created us and the universe. He went to the extreme measures of becoming human, walked among us, teaching us, healing people, and then dying in agony on the cross with all of our sins . . . just so we could be with Him forever in paradise!

Let's see, what choice should we make here? Should we believe a deceiver, who hates us and wants to ruin us? Or should we believe the eternal Creator-Lover who wants us to be happy and thrilled forever?

Ha! Like there really is a choice!


*Eph. 6:12    1 Tim. 4:1    Ps. 34:8*

# prayer 30

*Seducing Spirits*

Jesus, I can feel invisible forces tugging at my soul sometimes. They want to shoot false impressions at me regarding who You are.

I ask that You would so anchor me in relationship with You that no lie or false impression would stick to me. I want to be so in tune with You that the soil of my heart would be poison to any lying impressions that hell would try to plant within me.

Continue to reveal Your goodness and mercy to me every day. I want to be continually overcome with Your lovingkindness. Fill me with this truth and crowd out everything false.

[Continue praying in your own words.]

# Concept of Prayer 31
## *Slap Me Silly*

The pressures of life can often overwhelm us to the point that we forget to live.

Jesus promised us abundant life but many of us may feel that we've scored an F in the subjects of Fun 101 and the class of Fulfillment.

When we fall into a rut of any kind, we limit the huge dimensions of God's fabulous personality living out through us.  Of course, the entry point of salvation—the way of the Cross—is straight and narrow.  But once we enter God's Kingdom, the actual dimensions of His life are huge and endless—without confinement!

When our lives become cramped little boxes of repetition and sameness, we need to blow the walls out.  One of the best ways to break loose is to spend lots of time with people who know well the art of living.   God can bring into our lives friends who can inspire us with:

    (a)   industrial-strength joy and humor
    (b)   refreshing new ways of viewing life
    (c)   new adventures
    (d)   a positive "can-do" spirit
    (e)   all of the above

The danger is that we'll need to risk change.

*Neh. 8:10    Prov. 15:15    Prov. 4:18    John 10:10*

# prayer 31

## *Slap Me Silly*

God, I can so easily get obsessed with any number of things, whether it's business, finances, relationships, or whatever. And when I do, I get whacked off course.

Jesus, You promised abundant life. Where is it? My life is like a constant rerun of the same old same old. Help!

Give me new vision for my life. Give me grace to break through my fears and ruts.

Bring new people into my life that can escort me to new adventures that I would have never dared try on my own.

Bring a new sense of humor into my life. Deliver me from a bad case of serious.

[Continue praying in your own words.]

# Concept of Prayer 32
## *Pain Sensor*

What if God gave us a supernatural detector for where the pain is in the room?   The pleasure of pouring His love into people's pain is extraordinary.

How much fun could it be to see lives instantly changed as we deliver prophetic pictures or words that God gives to us?   They are the balm of Gilead to heal weary souls.

*Isa. 54:1-8    1 Pet. 3:8    Gal. 6:2    1 Thess. 5:14*

# prayer 32

## *Pain Sensor*

Jesus, please give me Your supernatural ability to know exactly who You want me to reach with Your love even if it happens while I'm at work, shopping, or in a restaurant. Create a sort of neon light over people You want me to speak to, and spell out for me what I'm supposed to give them.

I might not be great at this at first, but the more I just step out in faith, You'll perfect my sensitivity to what You're saying and to whom. I want to take that risk and encourage them with Your love.

Help me connect Your overwhelming provision with the needs of others, giving them hope and encouragement directly from Your heart, one person at a time.

[Continue praying in your own words.]

# Concept of Prayer 33
*Spiritual Photography*

The world's first photograph was produced by Joseph Niépce in 1826, but King David talked about photographic principles three thousand years ago. Speaking of God's ability to transfer His image to His people, David said, "As for me, I will be exposed to Your face in righteousness; I will be satisfied with Your likeness when I awake."

"Photography" means "writing with light." That process requires light-sensitive material to be exposed to light transmitted through a lens that brings the image into sharp focus.

Exposure to Jesus, (just like film or a digital chip is exposed to light) means that we receive the reward of His image being embedded into us.

The apostle Paul said, "But we all, with unveiled face beholding as in a mirror the glory of the Lord, are being transformed into the same image from glory to glory, just as from the Lord, the Spirit."

God is waiting to give us His light if we'll just focus and open up the shutter.

*Ps. 17:15     Rom. 8:29     1 Cor. 15:49     2 Cor. 3:18*

# prayer 33

## *Spiritual Photography*

Lord, I need more time just basking in the warmth of Your illumination, face to face.

I appreciate time spent in Bible study and prayer, but I'm determined to make more time for just being with You. "Doing" has its place, but true lovers are richly satisfied with just being together.

Please, Jesus, redefine for me the whole experience of being with You. Take me into a new dimension of being face-to-face with You. Help me make that happen on a consistent basis.

Show me what specific things are hindering my full exposure to Your illumination and image.

[Continue praying in your own words.]

# Concept of Prayer 34
*Hilarious Giver*

God's loves a hilarious giver. If that doesn't characterize our lives, no worries—God can create that kind of spirit in us. The enemy of hilarious giving is fear and unbelief. We can become paralyzed, unable to open our hand generously for fear that we'll become poor by giving to others. What's amazing is how the opposite is true! If we give freely, we'll receive freely. Conversely, if we hold back and hoard what we have, that's when financial stress and poverty will nip at our heels, or even consume us. God built that principle into the universe.

The extravagant promises of God for our outrageous blessings are activated by our giving. One of God's most intense promises for our wealth is attached to a very direct challenge in the book of Malachi. God told His people they had turned away from obeying His Word. He equated that with turning away from Him. He then said the road back to Him was to bring a full ten percent of their income into the storehouse. (For us, that's the church we attend). Giving a tithe, God says, is the way astounding blessing will come to us. Ignoring the tithe, however, opens the door for a financial curse.

The U.S. Department of Commerce released statistics on American churches. They reported the average church-attending household gives only $715 a year—about 2.4 percent of the average annual income. But if everyone in the church gave 10 percent—as God commanded us—what would that "tithe revival" look like as God poured out a blessing we can't contain?

*Mal. 3:7-10    Prov. 11:25    Luke 6:38    2 Cor. 9:7*

# prayer 34

## *Hilarious Giver*

God, Your Word says that You love a hilarious giver. Make me like that. Help me live out hilarious giving without any anxiety of what might happen if I give away generously.

Lord, I've withheld the tithe from my church. I confess that this is a violation of Your command to me. I know You're not legalistic, but You have reasons for requiring Your people to be givers.

Give me faith, Lord, to give ten percent of my income to my church. I need Your help and grace to do this! Work it in my heart.

Give me the spirit of hilarious giving. Make it become an exciting adventure instead of a burden.

[Continue praying in your own words.]

# Concept of Prayer 35
## *Drive-by Praying*

The Bible tells how people got healed simply when the apostle Peter's shadow fell on them. That didn't happen because he had a higher rank than we do in God's Kingdom. It happened in the Bible so we'd see that the guy who denied Jesus with cursing is the same man God used powerfully. Once God turned Peter around from his meltdown, he became central to the Book of Acts. God used ordinary people throughout the Bible in fantastic ways so we'd finally get the idea: "Oh yeah, God can even use *me*!"

A prayer doesn't have to be long to be effective. Nehemiah was a cupbearer to King Artaxerxes. One day while serving wine to the king, Artexerxes asked him why he was so sad. Nehemiah had just learned that Jerusalem lay in ruins. The king asked Nehemiah a history-making question: "What is your request?" Nehemiah prayed, then he told the king he wanted to rebuild the city. In that era, one walked delicately before majesty. Offending the king could cost you your life. So when the king asked his question, Nehemiah didn't fall to his knees and pray. It was more of an instant, inner, silent one-liner: "God, help!" That tiny prayer was answered, and it was critical to the entire nation of Israel.

We can say one-line prayers for people we see at a distance, even for a few seconds at a glance. They won't even know we're praying for them, yet we can become like snipers for Heaven. God can set in motion amazing things in their lives just from our tiny, instant prayers that we zap in their direction.

*Neh. 2:1-5   1 Cor. 4:20   John 16:24*

# prayer 35
## *Drive-by-Praying*

God, I'd like to get in the habit of saying one-line prayers for people I see at a distance, even if I just see them at a glance . . . like when I'm driving down the street and I see a jogger or a guy walking his dog.

I'm also asking that You'd give me boldness and desire to pray for friends and even strangers in public. It's a scary idea, but I don't want to be embarrassed if people see me praying for someone.

Since You're already inside me, I'm sort of like carrying You around places. Your treasure is in this clay jar (me) and since You come with me everywhere, I invite You to start doing outrageous things for people wherever I go.

[Continue praying in your own words.]

# Concept of Prayer 36
## *Theater from Hell*

Dark spiritual forces lie to us. It's not that we hear voices through our ears, but rather, impressions come as if by silent radiation bursting negative images about ourselves into our thoughts.

Lying spirits will throw film footage onto our mental theater screens showing us in the starring role of some horror movie. The film clips will play out tailor-made dramas proving how stupid we are, how ugly we are, how unloved we are, or whatever role that makes us feel most worthless and like giving up. The only acid bath that can totally dissolve those film clips is the spectacular truth of God's Word and our experiencing His unconditional love.

What we believe about ourselves is as powerful as physical DNA that demands an organism will be shaped like this or like that, and behaves in a specific manner. "As a man believes in his heart, so is he." So core value number one is the answer to the question "Who are we?" If we are born in Jesus, our identity is absolute: we've been born again in His image. It's a done deal. Our destiny is secured.

If we keep our hearts anchored to that spiritual reality, we will behave—almost without effort—according to that self-identity. The question is: are you wearing a "loser" hat? If so, why? Where did you buy it? Not from God's storehouse of truth!

*Prov. 23:7   Rom. 6:11   Rom. 8:29*
*Col. 2:6-8   1 Pet. 1:23   1 John 5:4*

# prayer 36

## *Theater from Hell*

God, I've been living my life as a person capable of sins and disastrous frailties; that's where my focus has been. And as a result, my self-view has perpetuated more and more bad behavior.

Please burn a new self-image into my heart, an image etched from who I truly am in You, born of Your Spirit and supported by Your grace.

When I came to faith in Jesus, You gave me new DNA—a new spiritual nature. Please infuse that into my emotions, my will, and my thoughts.

I want to walk out the power of a self-image that's created in Your truth, not stumble from believing lies about myself. Show me the lies I've believed, and replace them with how You see me, Jesus.

[Continue praying in your own words.]

# Concept of Prayer 37
*Religious Cookies*

God made each of us totally different from one another so that, by His Spirit, we would be unique expressions of His personality. Each of us has a capacity to reflect His glory like no one else.

Since He is the Creator of everything and has endless artistic genius, it wasn't His idea to generate so-called religious cookies: individuals who get stamped and baked into church people that all look and sound alike. Such can be the unintentional results of a religious culture.

In such a setting, men are taught to be safe and nice, while women are often suppressed and held back from various opportunities.

But wherever the Spirit of the Lord is, there's liberty. Wherever Jesus sets people free, they become more potently themselves than ever before possible. Wherever God works, new worlds come into existence. While religion tends to conform and regulate the masses, the Lord promotes, honors, and commissions individuals into unique adventures tailor-made just for them.

*1 Cor. 12:6     1 Cor. 12:17     1 Cor. 12:27-31*

# prayer 37

*Religious Cookies*

Lord, show me ways I've been bound by conformity and religion. Maybe I've been affected by the culture, my family, or simply by tons of dust settling over me through the course of living life the best I can.

Unbury me.

Catapult me to new ground.

I don't have to compromise my relationship with You as I become totally free in my own uniqueness. I want to glorify You through my specialized gift-mix and personality.

When the Holy Spirit moves through my liberated personality, talents and insights, people will be blessed by You more than ever!

You have something to give the world that can only come through me, and I need to receive that highly distinct honor from You in order to pass it on.

Holy Spirit, come move through my weaknesses, my quirkiness, and even my past failures, so the greatest number of people will be strengthened, inspired, and dazzled by You!

[Continue praying in your own words.]

# Concept of Prayer 38
## *The Claw In My Chest*

Everybody has at least one area of sinful weakness that so easily messes them up. It's like a claw that rips through all of our good intentions; the one thing that melts our resistance to sin like butter on a hot stove.

Over time, we can feel so beaten down by this one sin, we're tempted to give up. Or, we can ask Jesus for a totally new strategy from Heaven's war room.

God can give us the combination to the lock that has shackled us. That liberating combination to the lock of sin contains three things:

(1)     Asking the Holy Spirit to send us a personal email to our spirit—a very *specific promise* from God's Word—that packs the explosives we need to blow free;

(2)     Pursuing *intimacy* with Him often; and

(3)     Walking out *practical wisdom* of what God shows us—not just using the spiritual weapons of prayer, but taking steps toward freedom alongside friends who can supply added support.

One of the most practical ways to walk out of sin is to give room to doing the right thing. It sounds too simple, but the more we submit ourselves to God's Spirit and follow His leading, the more we'll become a slave to living free.

*Rom. 7:15     James 1:5     James 5:16*
*James 4:8     Heb. 12:1-6*

# prayer 38

## *The Claw In My Chest*

Jesus, I lift up to you the one area of sin that so often trips me up. I feel like a slave to it. This one sin almost feels omnipotent in my life, but I shout against it that *You* are the omnipotent One, and *You* want me free!

Please show me the key verses from Your Word that have the nuclear power to set me free.

Spending time soaking in Your presence is not easy with my schedule, but I continue to ask that You'd help me make it happen.

I also ask that You would give me the perfect friends and mentors to help me walk out of this thing victoriously.

I'm listening, and I'm waiting to act.

[Continue praying in your own words.]

# Concept of Prayer 39
## *World vs. Heaven*

Walking with Jesus is a dramatic journey, and any good drama involves conflict. Have you noticed that there's plenty of conflict involved in the faith walk? Not only are we dealing with internal conflicts from all of our personal baggage—freedom from which takes time, but we also have external conflicts and adversities in daily life. Add to that the fact we're at war, the spirit of this world being violently opposed to the Spirit of God in us and the message we carry.

We're deeply entrenched in this hostile world, yet our citizenship is in Heaven. So we literally live in two opposing realms simultaneously. When we spend so much time living at high speed in the secular world, in the business realm, at school, etc., we naturally get covered by "Earth dust," whereby unbelief seeps in. The world mindset is contagious, and it can give us a distorted perspective of the things of God. Of course, God intentionally chose to use foolish and weak things to confound the mighty. But we can get caught up with the high-minded stuff of the world, so that it can eclipse our view of God's awesome goodness and glory.

A fantastic goal would be to follow the example of men like Daniel. He had the amazing ability to be great in the world (a high government official) while being great in God's Kingdom (with childlike faith, a servant's heart, and friendship with God). He found the balance. Basically, we need to be like tea bags in hot water. The potency of tea leaves, packed with flavor and color, is so strong that it changes the water that surrounds the tea. The water doesn't cancel out the good stuff in the tea bag; on the contrary, the water gets changed by the tea.

*Dan. 6:16-28    Ps. 19:7    1 Cor. 1:23-27*

# prayer 39

## *World vs. Heaven*

Lord, I don't think of myself as worldly but this world does affect me—sometimes significantly.

I know You haven't called me to be a religious hermit or to be isolated. I need to be "in the world but not of it." Help me live out this balance.

Make me like Heaven's tea bag in the world.

I pray that You'd put the spirit of excellence on me in every area of life and work so that people would be drawn to me. I pray they'd taste the "tea of God" through me.

The one person in a crowded room who dominates the atmosphere is the person with the greatest passion. Eyes and ears turn to the one who has the fire.

I pray that You'd inflame my spirit with Your life.

[Continue praying in your own words.]

# Concept of Prayer 40
*Timing Is Everything*

Waiting for God's provision can sometimes go beyond mere suspense: it can tie your intestines into a fisherman's rapala knot.

God will often bring provision at the very last second to strengthen our faith. In the midst of faith-testing, it helps to remember that He's outside of time. He can set a specific provision in motion years before we need it so that it lands in our laps right on His cue at the very last second.

Jesus used a kid's lunchbox, turning its contents into enough food to feed five thousand people. He took what little the kid had—five loaves and two fish—and made it more than enough for a crowd. One moment, there was not enough provision; the very next moment, there it was . . . a miracle in motion.

The cool thing is, He did the miracle through the hands of the disciples. And then, after the disciples participated in that miracle, they ended up with more than they started with—twelve baskets of extra food! It was like one big gift basket for each disciple.

Is God good, or what?

*1 Kings 17:9-16    Matt. 14:14-21    John 16:24*
Matt. 17:24-27    Phil. 4:19

# prayer 40

*Timing is Everything*

Jesus, we desperately need provision and the waiting process is killing us!  Help!

I'm totally convinced that You're good and that You love us.  But I feel a little like the disciples riding with You through that violent storm.  They woke You up in a panic and said, "Don't You care that we perish?" Of course, You silenced the storm just in the nick of time.

It's not like we don't have a backlog of Your miraculous track record: You've done miracles nonstop in the Bible including raising the dead, healing the sick, paying taxes with a gold coin from a fish, feeding five thousand people out of a kid's lunchbox.

We have a long list of how You've come through with help and provision in our lives, too.  There have already been lots of miracles I have seen personally.

So help me to draw on the goodness of all that You've done in the past in order to trust You for today and tomorrow.  Could You please calm the storm inside me so I will trust You more peacefully?

[Continue praying in your own words.]

# Concept of Prayer 41
## *Change My Guts*

The human heart is clay; fragile at best.

Even after a terrific "up week," during which time we've soared high with spiritual inspiration, we may suddenly sense hard places in our heart—like little rocks. We can also feel like we're totally lousy at loving God, and traces of outright rebellion can emerge out of nowhere.

This is not always an immediate result of sin. The Lord works through pressure and heat in our lives to bring stuff to the surface, negative stuff that simply needs our conscious eviction.

Also, drawing closer to God's presence—that often has the effect of bringing heart issues to the surface. He just wants us to deal with these previously hidden areas. So it can actually be a good thing for bad things in our hearts to surface.

*Ps. 86:11    Ezek. 11:19    Matt. 22:37*

# prayer 41

## *Change My Guts*


Lord, thank you for bringing to the light hidden areas of my soul. Unite my heart to Yours so that all the parts within me, even the tiny areas way down, are in total alignment with Your Spirit.

What good is it if 90 percent of my heart is all out for God if I allow little anti-Christ pockets or points of idolatry to stay safely tucked away? So, with this level of honesty, I know You'll honor my request.

In addition to this, I want to love You consistently in two ways:

(1) I want to love You *without even trying* because You just keep pouring Your Spirit in me; and

(2) I want to use my willpower to love You with everything I've got, even when I'm going through really tough times. Of course, my effort to love You, by itself, is not great. I still need Your amazing grace in the mix.

I want the substance of my heart to soften and become receptive to Your slightest touch. Also, when You correct me, I want to sense Your eyes guiding me— I want us to be that close.


[Continue praying in your own words.]

# Concept of Prayer 42
## *Family Theme*

God is the Supreme Artist, and every artist deals with themes. His thoughts towards us and our families are more than the number of sand grains on the planet, and He knows the themes that He's purposed for our unique families.

The Lord gave a prophetic theme to each of the families or tribes of Israel. For centuries in Europe, they've had family crests and coats of arms—like thematic logos—to identify families.

If we know what God's theme is for our family, we can pray for it, nourish that theme, and align ourselves with it.

*Gen. 49:1-28    Jer. 29:11    Eph. 3:14-19*

# prayer 42

## *Family Theme*

God, show me what Your redemptive and prophetic theme is for my family. I'm already aware of the darker themes of my family—the weaknesses and pitfalls—but I need to know the glorious, too-good-to-be-true theme that You've destined to be the crest of our family.

Bring forth the positive family theme You have for us. And cancel out any negative family baggage in the process. I pray that You'd destroy the strategies of our spiritual enemies who would try to attack us in the very areas where You intend to bless us.

Open my eyes to the scarlet thread of Your work within the generations that came before me. Help me to intentionally cooperate with what You're about to do in our family unit now, and help me hand a brighter torch to those that follow after me.

[Continue praying in your own words.]

# Concept of Prayer 43
## *Heart Fabric*

Dishonest merchants have always been with us, and those in the first century developed tricks to make a few extra bucks at the expense of the customer. Some sellers of fabric virtually became magicians. They learned how to quickly unfold, flip and spin the fabric back and forth so it appeared perfect to the buyer, even though it had one or two big flaws in it. Customers thought they were seeing a perfect bolt of fabric, but they weren't seeing the bad parts. They bought the faulty cloth after being deceived.

Hearts can be like that flawed cloth. When we come to God in prayer, we can try to impress Him with our repentance and confession of sin, all while keeping certain key issues hidden, like those deceptive merchants did with their fabric. The absolute worst things buried in our hearts get cleansed and dissolved only when we bring them up to God—that really horrible stuff that we even hate admitting to ourselves.

The *crazy-dumb* thing is how we can think God doesn't see those things. But the *crazy-wonderful* thing is that when we're bare-bones honest with Him and bring those sins to the surface, we are set absolutely free!

*Jer. 17:9   Ps. 66:18   Ps. 32:5   Ps. 139:23*

# prayer 43

## *Heart Fabric*

Lord, I don't want to do to You the same thing those dishonest merchants did to their customers as they sold fabric. I don't want to hide the deep flaws and sins while I confess the easy stuff.

I know that my heart is self-deceptive and I don't always know what's down there. So turn the lights on way down deep.

You have no interest in condemning me. And as I see new stuff needing to be confessed, forgiven, and removed, I know that You're smiling at me through the whole process.

It might get messy, God, but I really want to be free.

[Continue praying in your own words.]

# Concept of Prayer 44
*Wet Plywood*

Adversity can come about in our lives through a number of core reasons:

(1)     God is testing our faith;

(2)     Our spiritual adversary is attacking us;

(3)     We are reaping from seeds we've sown;

(4)     Stuff just happens; and

(5)     A complex combination of all of the above.

When times get extremely intense, we'll never have a perfect schematic explaining the precise reasons everything is going wrong. But God knows the exact pathway of deliverance and breakthrough.

*2 Cor. 1:8-11    Col. 1:17    2 Sam. 22:3*
*Ps. 68:20    Ps. 59:17    Ps. 18:6-19*

# prayer 44

## *Wet Plywood*

Lord, the stress that I've been under is killing me. I feel like my molecules are coming apart. I literally feel like a sheet of plywood that has been thrown into a swimming pool and now the layers are coming unglued and warping.

I'm not sure why I feel so helpless. Most of my friends wouldn't believe I could get like this. I don't believe I've gotten like this. I feel like spiritual "raptors" are consuming me from the inside, while tons of pressures are hitting me from the outside. Help!

I know that by Your spoken Word, the molecules of the entire universe are held together. Please, hold me together now!

Take the darkness that's engulfing me and wear it like a large coat. Please come inside of my pain with me, so I'm not left wearing it all alone.

Be my anchor. Give me power from Your Spirit that takes care of the immediate unraveling that's going on. Then take my hand and bring me to a strong place. I need to become stronger, Lord, but I feel lost.

Rekindle my inner fire. Wrap me up in Your love. Make this agonizing time speed by and come to an end. Your mercies are new every morning, so I'm looking forward to what You're going to do next.

[Continue praying in your own words.]

# Concept of Prayer 45
## *Road Map*

We all know that we're supposed to walk by faith and not by sight, but does that mean we're supposed to stumble forward in ignorance and total darkness?

Faith is not a vacuum. Asking God for illumination and clarity is itself an act of faith.

Jesus is the way of salvation, of course, but He's also more: He's the path for every day, every moment.

What we often need is something like the map at the mall, the one displayed on a backlit kiosk featuring a big red dot labeled, You Are Here. Surrounding that red dot is a map of where all the stores are. We need something like that from God regarding our lives.

There are certainly seasons where we're walking with Jesus by faith through dense, uncertain darkness. But ultimately, we want to cooperate with the big picture that He has for us—a map of destiny that we want to see clearly, even if it's only one level at a time.

*John 14:6   Heb. 6:17-18   Heb. 12:1-2   Eph. 1:18*

# prayer 45

## *Road Map*

Lord, You are my Way all wrapped up in a person. Would You start to reveal to me where we're going in my life?

I pray that You'd use a spiritual yellow highlighter and start marking up important things You want me to see: specific things in Your Word, of course. But I also ask that You'd use anything and everything to grab my attention. Speak to me through other people and through various things so that I hear Your voice in surround sound, confirming and illuminating the current message You're speaking to me—rooted in the Scriptures, but amplified in daily life by the Holy Spirit.

And even though You are the Way of salvation, Jesus, I know that You are also the Way for every day of my life! The constant path of life for every moment is You! Let's do this!

[Continue praying in your own words.]

# Concept of Prayer 46
*Forgiveness*

There are times when it feels nearly impossible to forgive someone if we feel severely violated, betrayed, or deeply hurt.

But Jesus said that if we hold unforgiveness against anyone, it will result in our torment. That's not because God is hostile or unloving towards us, by any means; it's just one of those mechanisms built into the universe.

When we don't forgive someone, we're disagreeing with Heaven (the ultimate forgiving place) and agreeing with hell (the ultimate hateful place), so as a result, spiritual tormentors have legal access to our lives because it's like we put our arm of friendship around the shoulders of demons. It's a scary thought, but it doesn't have to be that way. God made every provision for all sin, and we need to agree with that . . . for ourselves and for others.

God has forgiven us a trillion dollars-worth of indebtedness that we owed because of our sin. So we simply can't get away with being unforgiving towards other people's hundred-dollar offenses—or even million-dollar ones.

Forgiving is not the same as agreeing that the offense done against us is okay. We don't have to become friends with those who have abused us. But when God said we should forgive "seventy times seven", He was likely acknowledging our occasional need to forgive that same person over and over as He works deep things in our hearts. His grace can help that forgiveness become permanent while He's healing our wounds.

*Matt. 18:21-35    Luke 11:4    Eph. 4:32    Col. 3:13*

# prayer 46

*Forgiveness*


God, I have a huge root of unforgiveness in me.

This is the big one. I haven't even wanted to forgive this person because I feel like they devastated me.

But I'm going to expose my hard heart to Your Cross. I'm going to obey You. I'm going to forgive everyone against whom I've had persistent unforgiveness.

Here are the names, God…

Lord, I totally release each person. They owe me nothing. Because You died to release them from every sin, I absolutely cannot hold them with unforgiveness. I totally forgive them, too.


[Continue praying in your own words.]

# Concept of Prayer 47
*Spiritual Sonar*

The Bible tells us that the whole world is under the sway of evil spiritual governments we can't see. God's Word also says that we are surrounded by a cloud of heavenly witnesses, and that the angelic armies who are for us are far more than those who are against us.

It also says that the spiritual realm is gigantic, highly sophisticated, and organized—beyond what our pea brains can comprehend. Both Heaven and hell have governmental structures, strategies, warriors, timetables, and weapons. And the whole theater of conflict is in rapid motion—both sides are literally at war with one another.

And yet, here we are on Earth, in the middle of it all, with most people believing hell doesn't exist and many folks timidly holding to some foggy notion of Heaven. Even some people of faith think of the spiritual dimension as static, irrelevant, and fairy tale-like. But the stakes of this spiritual war going on around us are tremendous! Many people equate the word "spiritual" with the concept of not-quite-real, and yet the spiritual realm is even more real than our cars!

Why doesn't God just destroy all the power of hell on earth right away? As humanity, we gave hell permission to rule on Earth through disobedience and sin. That critical point of understanding is explained in the Book of Genesis. Now hell is being evicted from Earth, one person at a time, one prayer at a time as the Kingdom of God flows through us.

*1 John 5:19   Eph. 6:12-18   Col. 2:15*
*2 Cor. 10:4   2 Cor. 2:11*

# prayer 47

## *Spiritual Sonar*

Lord, give me spiritual eyes. I need to see the riches I have in Christ. I need to fully recognize Your power. I need to value the inheritance I have in Heaven, and I need to understand the battle plans You have for my life . . . all while gaining understanding of the strategies of hell against me.

I sure don't want to dwell on the enemy's stuff, but I need You to give me spiritual sonar so that I can foresee wicked strategies formed against me—especially the incoming missiles of hell before they even get launched.

In the briefest moment, even while I'm brushing my teeth, You can suddenly give me a holographic flash in my spirit that reveals everything hell is plotting against me and how to move effectively against it with all of Heaven on my side.

[Continue praying in your own words.]

# Concept of Prayer 48
## *You're The Potter*

God is making us into His image—how cool is that? The challenge is that it requires our receptivity to His workmanship. Transition and transformation are processes usually requiring time, force, and cooperation on the part of the material being changed.

One analogy is how diamonds get formed out of coal. Something common, weak, flaky, and messy turns into a brilliant treasure that people wear on their fingers and around their necks because it's so gorgeous. It's also the hardest material on the planet.

Of course, for coal to become so glorious, the process is a little sobering. It takes 2,000 degrees Fahrenheit and 725,000 pounds per square inch of pressure to transform coal into a diamond over lots of time . . . and all of that happens about 100 miles down inside the earth. There's always a price for transformation.

God says in Isaiah, "Will the clay say to the potter, 'What are you doing?' Or the thing you are making say, He has no hands?'" When God's transforming work in our lives gets uncomfortable or costly, we can always rely on the fact that our IQ compared to His brilliance is like comparing the intelligence of a lump of clay to that of a master craftsman. God knows what He's doing, and His love for us is so extreme it's even self-sacrificing to the uttermost.

*Isa. 64:8    Jer. 18:4-6    Ps. 66:10*
*Job 23:10    Eph. 2:10    1 Pet. 1:3-9*

# prayer 48

*You're the Potter*

God, I can feel Your hand working change in my life. This process is really tough. I want to run from what You're doing. But I know that if I bail out of Your transforming process, I lose. Big time.

I know that You're taking the time and effort to shape me because You count me worthy of Your craftsmanship. And You value my destiny.

It would be horrible if I treated Your workmanship as having little value by resisting it or running from it.

I honor the work of Your hands in my life, God, even if it's coming at a great price.

Have Your way. I give you a blank check; You can do whatever You want. Please give me tons of grace for this process. And when I feel like it's getting more difficult than I can handle, give me glimpses of the glory that's ahead—the ultimate payoff of this whole process.

[Continue praying in your own words.]

# Concept of Prayer 49
## *Less Is More*

Pruning is a weird agricultural process because we cut back branches from trees that are already fruitful, and we do this to get even more fruit out of them. That's bizarre. Something good is taken away so that, in the long run, more of something better will come forth.

Since God designed everything in creation for a purpose, He obviously built things into nature to illustrate spiritual truths.

So how does pruning work in *our* lives? God cuts something away so that the very area that experienced temporary loss—by His hand—ends up getting even more fruitful.

God is a genius!

*Matt. 16:25    John 15:2    Matt. 19:29*

# prayer 49

*Less Is More*

Lord, I don't want to resist pruning, because I know that if I try to save my life, I'll lose it; but if I lose it for Your sake, I'll find it.

Holy Spirit, keep reminding me of this! It feels scary, but I'm determined to trust Your goodness.

God, I only want more and more and more in the long run, even if it means *less and less* in the short term! Prune my life, Lord, so that I can explode with blossoms, fruit, and stronger branches!

[Continue praying in your own words.]

# Concept of Prayer 50
## *Tuning Fork*

It's really cool how someone can sing into a piano and the strings will sing back by resonating with the same pitch of the voice, vibrating with the same exact frequency.

What's really awesome is to realize that Jesus, the One who made Heaven and Earth—along with billions of galaxies—is the very One who rejoices over us . . . *with singing and shouts of joy!*

It would be hard to believe this if His Word didn't make that very proclamation! He really does sing over us with joy!

*Zeph. 3:17    Ps. 29:8    Heb. 12:26*

# prayer 50

## *Tuning Fork*

Lord, You sing over me with joy!

I want to hear that song. In fact, I want the vibration of Your voice, singing over me, to come down and shake the Earth. I want everything in my life to resonate with that specific vibration of Your song over me.

I want everything in my world to shake with heavenly designs of order, restoration, and awesome breakthroughs, because Your songs over me are real, and they have breath, and they have resonance—even a frequency like an earthquake.

Vibrate every cell of my being and shake everything in my life with Your song! Force my spiritual enemies to hear that song loud and clear, and as they do, wipe them out by Your musical celebration over me.

[Continue praying in your own words.]

# Concept of Prayer 51
*Season*

God made different seasons for our planet. And spiritually speaking, we're supposed to be full of life all the time, in season and out of season.

Even when a Winter season comes into our lives, we need to remember that God's gifts are still current and operative. His grace, goodness, and miracles are ever-present, unaffected by seasons.

But whenever we do experience a personal winter, a whole lot of things in life that we love may seem to lose their blossoms and leaves. Things can almost appear to enter a sort of death. It's good to remember that the seasonal cycle is going to come right back around again, and it will be Spring before long.

God can help us recognize the season He's working in our lives at any given time. Creation encourages us that seasons end with transition to the next stage of His wonderful plan.

*2 Tim. 4:2    Eph. 5:16    Gal. 6:10*
*Prov. 6:6-11    Prov. 12:24*

# prayer 51

*Seasons*

God, help me through the Winter seasons when things aren't blooming. I need to be a person who is constantly sowing into the future, whether it's by developing a side business, learning a new skill, networking with people, or whatever it may be at Your leading.

Help me learn to wisely use small increments of time—maybe even by getting up an hour early each day—so that as the months and years pass, I will have accomplished awesome things by sowing toward the next Spring and harvest time according to Your purposes.

[Continue praying in your own words.]

# Concept of Prayer 52
## *I Want To Live Outrageously!*

Obeying God's Word is not a heavy burden, by any means! Rather, it's the gateway to life. And when a person continually walks in super-abundant life, it's fun, fulfilling, and explosive! Three clusters of amazing promises for outrageous blessing are linked to three key actions on our part:

(1)     If we embrace God's Spirit, and His Word dwells in our hearts and our speech, and if we pass this wealth on to our future generations, then here are the results:

> —His glory rises over us;
> —He will gather us into family relationships;
> —We'll be radiant with joy; and
> —Our hearts will thrill at His abundance.

(2)     If we trust in God, and if we take intimate refuge in His presence, as if right under His wings, then:

> —He will deliver us from evil and all fear;
> —He will make sure evil doesn't win against us;
> —He will send lots of angels to protect us;
> —He will crush our enemies under our feet;
> —He will answer us when we call; and
> —He will satisfy us with a good, long life.

(3)     If we freely give, help set people free, take care of the homeless and the helpless, and give ten percent of our income to God's storehouse (the church), then:

> —He will pour out a blessing that overflows;
> —He'll smash any devourer that would hurt us;
> —He will make us recover fast;
> —His glory will cover us; and
> —Our gloom will shine like the noonday sun.

*Isa. 59:21 - 60:9     Ps. 91     Isa. 58:6-10*
*Mal. 3:10-12     Luke 6:38*

# prayer 52

## *I Want to Live Outrageously!*

Lord, as I obey Your Word, please unleash Your awesome blessings upon me so I can become an even greater blessing to everyone else!

Blow the lid off of life as I've known it. Tear down walls that have kept me away from Your blessings and miraculous provision.

Help me to memorize Your Word so that I'll be radiant with joy;

Help me take refuge in Your intimacy often so that Your abundant protection and fulfillment will take place;

Help me give freely to the poor and to tithe to my church so that You'll pour out a blessing that I can't even contain, and Your glory will cover me.

Help me, God, to escape mere surviving, living by default, or being stuck in any rut. Help me to live outrageously!

[Continue praying in your own words.]

# Part Three

## A Theology of Intimacy

### *Nose to Nose with the Almighty*

Not long ago, my wife and I found ourselves in an amazing little country church. It provided a very casual atmosphere, but appearances can be deceiving. The place was absolutely electrified with God's presence.

The grade-school kids were learning how to prophesy with absolute accuracy. People were being instantaneously healed from broken bones, tumors, HIV, you name it. And the Word was taught with incredible insight.

This church was like a breath of fresh air, although my wife and I had personal adjustments we needed to make within this new kind of church environment.

As for me, I soon discovered pockets of religiousness within my own heart.

On one particular occasion, the worship leader, a young man with a guitar, was calling out a prayer with a loud voice, "Lord, we *pull* on You! We *pull* on You, today, God!"

In response to his unbridled call, a tiny pocket of religious superiority surfaced in me. After all, I'm a Bible college graduate, and I know stuff. So, I whispered inwardly to myself, *This certainly isn't the appropriate way to address the Almighty, "We pull on You." I wonder if we really belong in this church, after all?*

Right away, I perceived the Holy Spirit coming face-to-face with me saying, "Bob, do YOU pull on Me?" He asked this with the sweetest tenderness, yet His words burned into my bone marrow.

I was stunned, and stared back into this invisible eye contact with God, gazing like a witless deer at headlights. I finally gathered up enough wisdom to reply, "Yes, God. I *do* pull on You."

Those words of agreement were soon on my lips, as I called out, along with everyone else, an energetic invitation for God to show up in the meeting, and for Him to enter our hearts in a fresh way.

That incident became one of the most important spiritual lessons I've ever learned. It's interesting to note that when Jesus corrects one of the churches in the Book of Revelation, and when God addresses the nation of Israel repeatedly throughout the Old Testament, the theme that seems to be foremost on His heart is how His people tend to forget their first-love relationship with Him, and how they often play the harlot by following idols. (What's one possible contrast to acting as prostitutes? Being faithful in marriage, perhaps?)

If this kind of close relationship is so consistently important to the Lord, maybe it needs to be important to all of us.

The word "religion" is the ultimate baggage word. It's a gigantic holding tank because of the millions of different associations and meanings it holds for billions of people. Religion carries with it life-giving values to many while representing painful personal baggage to others, even death to some. "Religiousness", as I'm using it, is the industrial-strength version of human religious zeal functioning on its own steam apart from God.

The scary thing about religiousness (something we're all vulnerable to) is how effectively it can take living spiritual truth and squash the very life out of it— all while a halo of self-bequeathed virtue adorns the head. Religiousness then handles that spiritual truth with the utmost reverence, as if it were a precious artifact—like a Monet painting—and gently nails that beautiful truth (now devoid of any dynamic life) high up on the wall, beyond the reach of common folks. It doesn't just hang the truth crudely from a nail, but rather it mounts that once-alive truth within a beautiful ornate frame glorified by the gilded title, "Homage and Respect."

That's a picture of what religiousness does to God's truth. It kills it and then enshrines it. Then with theatrical skill, it maintains the appearance of utmost respect for God's Word while slamming the door closed on God's Spirit and the intimacy that God craves to have with His people. To make things worse, through the assistance of fallen human nature, the mechanics of religiousness tend to keep *other* hungering people from entering into that intimacy with Him as well.

The following two diagrams delineate a common tendency of human nature. One shows the chemistry of Religion vs. God and the other shows the dynamics between Religion vs. the Holy Spirit.

# Religion vs. God
## (Story Paradigm)

PHARISEES SEE THEMSELVES AS "PROFESSIONAL GOD PEOPLE"

GOD SHOWS UP IN HUMAN FLESH

"PROFESSIONALS" DRIVEN BY: POSITION POWER & PRIDE

GOD CHALLENGES THE CORE VALUES OF THE PROFESSIONALS

CORE VALUES:
--NOT INTIMACY WITH GOD
--RATHER, THE PRESERVATION AND ENFORCEMENT OF LAWS

"THE PROFESSIONAL GOD PEOPLE" ARE THREATENED: THEY WANT TO KILL GOD

# Religion vs. The Holy Spirit
(Story Paradigm)

RELIGIOUS-DRIVEN THEOLOGIANS SEE THEMSELVES AS "PROFESSIONAL GOD PEOPLE"

GOD SHOWS UP IN MIRACULOUS MANIFESTATIONS OF THE HOLY SPIRIT

"PROFESSIONALS" DRIVEN BY: DOCTRINES DEFINITIONS & DEBATES

GOD CHALLENGES THE CORE VALUES OF THE "PROFESSIONALS" VIA CHILD-LIKE FAITH OF ORDINARY PEOPLE

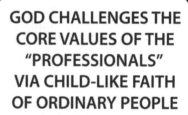

CORE VALUES:
--<u>NOT INTIMACY WITH GOD</u>
--RATHER, ASSOCIATION WITH GOD AT A SAFE DISTANCE THROUGH THEOLOGY

"THE PROFESSIONAL GOD PEOPLE" ARE THREATENED: THEY WANT TO DISCREDIT TESTIMONIES ABOUT THE CURRENT WORK OF THE HOLY SPIRIT

The conflict between religiousness and the Holy Spirit played out dramatically in the Book of Acts with a wise man named Stephen, a man of good reputation who was filled with the Holy Spirit and who was working powerful signs and wonders among the people.

Before long, a particular religious sect started making false accusations against him. This group of zealots stirred up the elders and the scribes to a frenzy, and the mob dragged Stephen before the Council. The high priest asked Stephen if all these accusations were true.

In response, Stephen recited an excellent history lesson of how God had been working among His people for generations. He concluded with a very strong rebuke to the religious community—a confrontation which cost him his life:

> You men who are stiff-necked and uncircumcised in heart and ears are always resisting the Holy Spirit; you are doing just as your fathers did. Which one of the prophets did your fathers not persecute? And they killed those who had previously announced the coming of the Righteous One, whose betrayers and murderers you have now become; you who received the law as ordained by angels, and yet did not keep it.          **—Acts 7:51 - 53**

Within minutes, they were stoning him to death.

One of the angrier moments Jesus displayed in the Gospel accounts is when He said:

> But woe to you, scribes and Pharisees, hypocrites, because you shut off the kingdom of heaven from men; for you do not enter in yourselves, nor do you allow those who are entering to go in.
> **—Matt. 23:13**

The Kingdom of Heaven is not just salvation, it's the entire Kingdom, including everything God promised us. It's the realm of God's rulership, treasures, gifts, and relationships.

So when Jesus urges His people to remember their first-love relationship with Him—the one thing He doesn't want His people to ever forget—does that sound like a theological precept begging for a debate? Or does it sound like a plea for personal intimacy that's begging for a personal response?

The Scriptures keep repeating the fact that God longs to have a very close relationship with us, something akin to the honeymoon of a husband and wife. And such relationships are all about *response*—at every level (Isa. 62:5, Song of Solomon, Matt. 11:16-19, Rev. 19:7).

### *The Secret of the Universe*

When the Holy Spirit confronted me about my adverse reaction to the worship leader's words of "pulling on the Lord," I was convicted of my own religiousness. What I was dealing with was truth ("We should revere God") that had somehow gotten petrified and converted into a religious stone within my heart, resulting in a wall of hindrance ("Don't you dare draw THAT close to Him!").

Religiousness is an enemy of intimacy with God, and it's also an enemy of creativity and freedom. In a religious environment, everything needs to be screwed down to the floor with legalistic force—just this side of stripping the threads off the screws—so that human control can be established in the name of God. Usually it's a hierarchy of elite authority existing to enforce a preferred worldview. Such a mindset may say:

*We can't trust the ordinary people to be too powerful and become too free in God; that could get really messy. And, really, we can't trust the process of God to effectively work through ordinary, unqualified, unschooled people either (without the elite in control) because, well, these are evil times, and who knows what error or damage could result. Bad things could happen, things God certainly wouldn't want, and so we need to help protect God from such calamity by enforcing our structures.*

The Pharisees of Jesus' time excelled at this virtuous heroism . . . "protecting" God from danger. They killed Him in the process, of course, but their religious zeal was impressive as they sought to keep the law intact and to keep everything screwed down tightly to the floor.

Let me affirm the fact that I absolutely treasure excellent systematic theology. Presented by richly educated men and women who love God and who love people, and whose skill sets enable them (with the craftsmanship of Mercedes-Benz engineers, as it were) along with Holy Spirit anointing—nothing's better. Such people can relate to the common folks the profound things of God so that the revelations are totally clear, compelling, and engaging, resulting in an abundance of fruitfulness and godliness in people's lives. Such a scenario exemplifies a rich faith *not* driven by fear of losing control.

The real caveat comes when that megatrend of frail human nature is allowed to demote the true dynamics of Scripture downward into the realms of unbelief, compromise, and humanly managed God-contact.

Sound doctrine and systematic theology are critical. They are the foundations of our faith. They do need to be guarded against error. We do need to rightly divide the Word because it can be divided wrongly, too.

So where do we often go wrong?

Let's talk about foundations. My marriage has many foundations: commitment, communication, love, wedding vows, civil laws, and God's laws, among others. Another foundation we enjoy is the concrete footings and floor joists under our master bedroom. I won't go into details, but I'm sure it would be no shock to anyone that my wife and I enjoy intimacy with one another. The setting of this intimacy is the bedroom. That bedroom has its own array of foundations that must be in place for the sake of our relational intimacy.

However, I am not in love with the 2x4s, floor joists, or footings that provide a foundation needed for romance between my wife and myself. But they do have their place and are a crucial component of the structure of things.

Systematic theology and sound doctrine is part of the foundation of our relationship with God so that intimacy between us and God can take place. What's really weird is that people can actually begin to worship theology. The human heart can fall into "bibliolatry," whereby the Bible becomes our focus of relationship and affection, instead of God. That's what happened to the Pharisees. Their knowledge of God's Word gave them power over people, but it wasn't God's true power born of love to serve people in truth.

Good people in good churches with effective authority structures in place, of course, have tremendous value. And High Church cultures, that give to us visual representations of the things of God as well as traditions and sacred rituals, can be extremely edifying. Not long ago, I was spiritually uplifted during a fabulous service in an Episcopal church that displayed a wide array of physical artifacts, banners, priestly attire, swinging incense urns, and a well-planned liturgy. And through these things, the place was brimming with spiritual vitality.

Although "God is not religious, but relational", mankind is both. The actual word "religion" (*threskeia*) is rare in the New Testament; it is used to contrast good religion and bad religion. It is interesting how James, the half-brother of Jesus, describes the two kinds:

> "If anyone thinks himself to be religious, and yet does not bridle his tongue but deceives his own heart, this man's religion is worthless. This is pure and undefiled religion in the sight of our God and Father, to visit orphans and widows in their distress, and to keep oneself unstained by the world."
> **—James 1:26, 27**

There is a religion God approves—godly practice and piety (*eusebeia* – "godliness/godlikeness") which God accepts as pure and faultless.

God is not against religion. He is against the wrong kind. Both Scripture and Church history bear witness to both kinds of religion, and it is wisdom to affirm this reality. The problem emerges when religion takes center stage and eclipses the priority of personal, intimate relationship with God. Religion also becomes a problem when it becomes a manmade tool used to skillfully edit God according to preference.

For example, Scripture says, "And God has appointed in the church, first apostles, second prophets, third teachers, then miracles, then gifts of healings, helps, administrations, various kinds of tongues" (1 Cor. 12:28). A religious culture can often take a verse like that and hand-pick the items it wants on its shopping list (teachers, helps, and administrations) while editing out others (prophets, miracles, healings, and tongues) putting those into a separate file labeled, "No Longer Needed Today, But Thank You."

The apostle Paul is indicating in the above verse that miracles, healings, and tongues should obviously be flourishing within a safe and organized setting provided by apostles, prophets, and teachers. But authority should be in place within the Church not to control, edit, and rule over the common folks and their spiritual gifts, but to support, serve, nourish, and honor them all.

Without question, the living church needs organizational and foundational structures in place so that things of life can get communicated and accomplished. A good illustration is how we need structure in the human body (our skeleton) for the support of otherwise flaccid or amorphous tissues and organs so they, in turn, can function and keep us alive.

If our religious structure becomes the main deal, however, it's just as if the human skeleton were to become the main deal. If the human body featured its skeleton as the most prominent attribute, it would be shrouded with an exoskeleton (a skeleton on the outside of our body). That's how insects proudly display their skeletons, outwardly and prominently.

So if a church does the same thing, and its structure and organization and programs become the main deal, it would be emulating the style of insects. And what might the behavior be of so-called religious insects whose structures and programs become the main deal? They would scurry about with organized activity solely to keep the colony organized so that they could continue to scurry about with organized activity solely to keep the colony organized, etc., ad infinitum. Hence, a very dry existence.

Most of the major denominations in existence today were originally started by an outrageous move of the Holy Spirit, complete with signs, miracles, and wonders as found in the Book of Acts. Those historical documents are hard to find, but they do exist. (I sense another book coming over me.)

Back to my own religiousness of heart, which got lovingly stung by the Holy Spirit in church when the worship leader called out to God that we were "pulling" on Him.

That was a defining moment for me. It has since come to represent or distill the best of the best of what I've learned from having walked with the Lord for thirty-eight years. It even goes beyond any one specific thing I can remember learning in Bible college, though the sum total of that education is valuable beyond measure.

This one revelation (pulling on God) could best be articulated by one small statement. But let me warn you, it utilizes a current colloquialism that some folks might find offensive. Please know that my intent is not to be offensive, but rather to simply express the beauty of a scriptural truth.

The most important thing I've learned so far, after decades with Jesus, is:

"The Kingdom of God belongs to people who suck."

Let me give you a quick explanation, before this book is hurled across the room and against a wall.

# 1. Babies Suck.

As a result, while nursing at the breast, babies get milk. No suction, no milk. When people go to church, it may often be the case that many walk through the door without a violent determination to desperately "suck", (that is, PULL), from the Lord everything He's got for them, everything promised in the Bible, each Sunday.

To do that, it takes hunger. Babies get hungry, so they suck. Conversely, folks who attend church may not be hungry, so they don't suck. Multiply that complacency throughout the congregation of any given church, over years or decades, and you get a concentrated church experience akin to day-old oatmeal, something that really doesn't excite anyone. Non-faith people certainly have no desire to endure that punishment. But the "faithful" still go, because they believe that's what you're supposed to do to make God happy.

After all, it is reasoned, doing something that's not enjoyable, like suffering through stale church services, is one more way to prove that we're really serving God as we function from a gut-level endurance born of faith. And that's a virtue, isn't it?

I mean, if church were full of awesome wonders and supernatural enjoyment all the time, we might not be able to *prove* our religious fortitude displayed through the suffering of endurance. We might be having way too much doggone fun in His presence, and that wouldn't be right, would it?

In the midst of a stagnate church venue (a place in which people don't diligently seek His face), people may often think or say, "We can do church just fine without anything miraculous happening, thank-you-very-much. After all, we are people who walk by *faith*, not by *sight!*"

This, of course, is a brilliant inversion of Bible truth. Signs and wonders are actually *supposed* to accompany people who believe, the Scriptures say (Mark 16:17, Acts 5:12, Heb 2:3-4). Then again, people who *don't* want the power of God or His manifest presence will not only justify their lukewarm distance, but will also pride themselves with the idea that, somehow, their walking "by faith" is actually most honorable when it can be done just fine without any "crutch" that God might otherwise give to "weaker" folks . . . "crutches" such as miracles, healings, or supernatural gifts—those wonderful things He's promised to us in His Word.

What a slap in His Face!

Imagine friends and family doing that to us at Christmas time: physically hurling back our presents at us, maybe hitting us right in the eye!

# 2. Sometimes life sucks.

Most depressed people who are high on drugs or lying low in the gutter realize that their lives suck. They often say as much. People whose lives are in a disastrous mess usually know all too well, without anyone telling them, that their lives are in a state of depravity or desperation. Such people don't have to be convinced that their lives suck. That's often the state of being wherein many people realize their need for God.

By contrast, people who clothe themselves in religiousness or self-sufficiency are not often in touch with their depravity at all, but are instead like fancy coffins filled with cold bones—appearing religious but without any hunger, love, or dynamic life. (I think of my religious neighbor who tortured me throughout childhood. I also think of myself, sitting in church, piously muttering that we shouldn't be "pulling on God.")

Jesus told a wonderful story about this in the eighteenth chapter of Luke. There was a very religious man, a Pharisee, who stood next to a sinful man inside the temple. The religious Pharisee gave a verbally flourishing prayer to God, thanking Him that he was not like other, sinful people, especially not like the sinful tax collector standing right next to him. (Tax collectors were typically known for stealing people's money). The religious man's prayer continued on, recounting all of the great religious acts and virtues that he felt he had racked up, like merit points, before God.

Near him, the sinful man stood in shame. He felt so horrible about his sense of ungodliness that he couldn't even raise his eyes to God. He started hitting his own chest for emphasis while praying, "Be merciful to me, God, I'm a sinner. *I totally suck!*" [Italics are my paraphrase.]

Jesus said that this tax-man sinner was the guy who was justified before God, and he was forgiven that day, *not* the religious man with all of his ritualistic ornaments and peacock feathers stitched arduously in place attesting to his self-proclaimed godliness. God simply wasn't impressed.

The Kingdom of God belongs to people who suck—that is, people who seek His face continually (Ps. 105:4).

A third example of how the Kingdom of God belongs to people who suck, though from a totally different perspective...

# 3. Science and Suction—
# A Spiritual Symbolism.

Here is another example of how a different kind of suction illustrates the Kingdom of God. Let me present this observation as more of a grade-school science lesson, if you will, weaving alternately between the scientific and the spiritual counterpart.

## Science:

Suction is what makes a siphon work. The technical term is "hydrostatic pressure." That's the pressure exerted on a column of fluid as a result of the weight of the fluid above it.

Spiritual:

Heaven is packed with God's love, mercy, gifts, provisions, power, superabundance, and much more, all of which He yearns to give away and to overflow into the lives of hungry and hurting people. God's perfect love is so compassionate, He urgently wants to freely give away great stuff wherever there is hunger, pain, and need (low-pressure areas on Earth, if you will). Therefore, the atmosphere of Heaven (the weight of the fluid above) is characterized by exceedingly high pressure, while the Earth has a very low atmospheric pressure.

Because Earth has this low-pressure atmosphere in terms of heavenly abundance (actually, a vacuum-like atmosphere of lack), God looks for ways to invade Earth with His superabundance; therefore, He's looking for conduits.

Science:

The conduit in our science lab, a rubber hose, is what contains the column of fluid. Remember, pressure is exerted on that column of fluid in the rubber hose as a result of the weight (or pressure) of the fluid above it. So once there's been priming suction on the hose to get the flow going (if necessary), the weight above takes over, and a rich flow emerges.

Spiritual:

As people suck, that is, pull on the Lord because they are hungry and because they seek His Face, His Power, His presence, and His gifts to become manifest, this begins a flow from Heaven to Earth.

Consequently, God is looking for people who value Him enough to pull on Him and to prime the siphon. Such people become living conduits of Light-Water, or a love-flow from Heaven to Earth.

Here are a few Scriptures pertaining to this idea:

"For the eyes of the LORD move to and fro throughout the earth that He may strongly support those whose heart is completely His."                    **—2 Chron. 16:9**

"Blessed are you who hunger now, for you shall be satisfied."                    **—Luke 6:21**

"He has filled the hungry with good things; and sent away the rich empty-handed."
                    **—Luke 1:53**

"Thy kingdom come. Thy will be done, on earth as it is in heaven."        **—Matt. 6:10**

"And from the days of John the Baptist until now the Kingdom of Heaven suffers violence, and violent men take it by force."
                    **—Matt. 11:12**

"Violence / force" = Pulling and sucking

Because this may be a totally new concept to some, let's underscore and review just a bit. The force in Heaven that wants to push downward toward Earth includes the compassion, riches, gifts, salvation-already-purchased, glory, and love that God yearns to pour upon everyone on the planet. But He is looking for rubber hoses or living conduits, that is, people who suck—people whose hearts are totally after Him.

These are folks who are desperately hungry for Him far more than those people who are already satisfied with their self-sufficiency or religion (the rich in Luke 1:53, the ones God sent away empty-handed).

This has nothing to do with denominations. It has nothing to do with being Presbyterian or Baptist, nor does it have anything to do with Protestants vs. Catholics. It has everything to do with being human individuals with human hearts.

I know several people ministering in Africa and the Middle East who are discovering more and more Muslims who have been very hungry for God. Some have consequently had dreams whereby Jesus has approached them and revealed His salvation. Many were consequently waking up born again and totally ecstatic about their new faith. God was searching for hungry hearts, and He found them.

By the reports that have come to my ears, God reaching Muslims in this miraculous fashion seems to be going on constantly across the globe, and it appears that the numbers of such instances are increasing rapidly.

When any people begin to pull on Heaven because they are both hungry themselves and hungry on behalf of others, God takes serious notice. And the siphon process, in one form or another, begins as they call out to Him.

As the hose freely conducts the water from above to below, it shares the water it receives from above. It distributes it—or administers it—and this perpetuates the suction that draws more into the hose. As the hose continues to give away its water flow from the vast resource above it, the more that hose keeps getting re-supplied.

If the hose were to pinch itself off, worried about giving away too much of its precious water, it wouldn't receive any more from the source above and the Heaven-flow would stop.

The more that a person "tastes and sees that the Lord is good" (Ps. 34:8), there grows a dual craving: a passion to get more of God for one's self, but also an equal, if not stronger, passion to share Him with others.

> "The generous man will be prosperous, and he who waters will himself be watered."
> **—Prov. 11:25**

> "Give, and it will be given to you; good measure, pressed down, shaken together, running over, they will pour into your lap. For by your standard of measure it will be measured to you in return."    **—Luke 6:38**

So the more you get of God, the more you want of Him; the more you want of Him, the more you get. In the midst of all that, the passion to give Him away gets extremely intense.

To enter into this kind of ongoing "Heaven on Earth" dimension of faith, we need to get new wineskins for the new wine that God wants to give us. If we seek God for this, we're not going to end up with an evil spirit. Knowing our paranoia over such things, Jesus actually made a point of covering this issue in Luke 11:12-13, saying that if a father is asked by his son for an egg, will he hand the kid a scorpion?

> "If you then, being evil, know how to give good gifts to your children, how much more shall your heavenly Father give the Holy Spirit to those who ask Him?"
> **—Luke 11:13**

We will not fall into heresy by asking God for things He's already promised to us in the Bible. Heresy is to say something like "Jesus isn't God." Heresy is to say something like, "The blood of Jesus doesn't cleanse away sin." Heresy is NOT saying things like, "All the miracles Jesus did we can do also, and greater, because He promised us that!"

Heresy is NOT saying, "Let's get as much of the Holy Spirit as possible, even if we get drunk like they did in Acts 2, then we'll go out to the shopping mall and speak the encouragement of God's love over people and ask God to heal them! It'll be so much fun!"

> "Heal the sick, raise the dead, cleanse the lepers, cast out demons; freely you received, freely give."                              **—Matt. 10:8**

> "And no one puts new wine into old wineskins; otherwise the new wine will burst the skins, and it will be spilled out, and the skins will be ruined. But new wine must be put into fresh wineskins."
> **—Luke 5:37-38**

### *All You Have To Do Is Ask*

Hunger for God is not something that comes naturally to any of us. So, if you do a quick soul-search and find none, don't despair—just ask. Ask a lot! I ask all the time. That doesn't make me "spiritual," rather it reveals just how human and desperate I am. And we're all made of the same clay. The only thing is, we have to be *motivated* to keep asking God to give us an urgent hunger for Him and to give us a love for people. Asking is so easy, and yet it really does take effort—to actually do it, I mean.

### *Supernatural Is Natural*

I've written the previous pages to show you the kind of spiritual odyssey I've been on which gave rise to this book of fifty-two very simple but outrageous prayers.

The power of these prayers is not resourced in their eloquence or profundity by any means. The power comes from the fact that they simply connect ordinary people with a miraculous God, hopefully providing a new spark of inspiration of faith. Also, these fifty-two prayers may connect people to topics of prayer they may have never thought of before, or maybe they just never dared pray about before.

These prayers also serve as priming pumps. You should feel free to pray the printed prayers verbatim, then continue praying in your own words concerning the topic or theme presented.

If folks just start praying boldly, with newfound permission, according to Scripture, I believe many are going to start having their socks blown off by one mighty miraculous wind as All Power shows up! (John 14:12; Acts 2:2)

I'm going to end with one more account of God's miraculous power. It may not appear quite as spectacular as the others I've shared, nor does it seem particularly spiritual . . . and that's just the point. It illustrates how God operates in the workplace, a topic which I believe to be very important. We need to experience the supernatural everywhere, all the time, so that the most number of people can benefit. I'm also sharing this account because there could be a temptation for some readers to feel that there's been so much emphasis in this book on the supernatural, that real-world issues have somehow been minimized. The chief point I want to drive home, however, is that when Heaven comes to Earth, all kinds of solutions and provisions pour forth, whether it involves feeding orphans or avoiding disaster on a film project.

In sharing this story, I felt it necessary to include plenty of technical details to paint the picture of how urgently God's intervention was needed by my business partner and myself as filmmakers, even when we didn't really know how much we needed Him to cover our backsides. It's important to recognize how effectively God can intervene in secular or non-spiritual settings. Actually, because He made *everything*, I believe it's a bit loony to even have a distinction between sacred and secular, since God is in all and through all. But I suppose the need for such distinction is sometimes practical.

### *"Lights, Camera, God!"*

My business partner and I have enjoyed wonderful adventures in our film production company. We've won awards and had a lot of very happy clients. We've seen God's provision come through for us in many ways over the years. One particular moment of miraculous intervention stands out in my mind.

We were hired to do a film with a running time of five minutes and sixteen seconds. The budget was about $2.5 million. The project was a theme park "ride-film," that took us a year and a half to produce with a small army of technicians.

The film was so expensive (about $8,000 per running second) because it was very complicated: it was a 3-D movie with film footage that came straight out of super-computers at high resolution (4,000 lines), running at 30 frames per second, printed onto Vista-Vision film with a Celco film recorder and then bumped to 70mm. Two 70mm movie projectors were required in the theater, one for the left eye and another for the right eye. Polarizing glasses would be worn by the audience.

The film also involved optical effects and live-action footage shot from a helicopter. The film's theater in Japan had a fifty-five foot wide screen and the show utilized synchronized motion-controlled audience seats custom made by Mitsubishi just for our project. There was a synchronized eleven-track digital discrete sound system, in-house smoke and laser effects, and audio-animated characters.

Time was a critical issue. Our film absolutely had to open on December 3, which was a special anniversary for the city in Japan where this $700 million theme park was built. Government officials would be in attendance to officiate its opening. Our film was one of the four main attractions.

We could NOT miss this deadline!

Eighty percent of the film we were making was heavily dependent on the computer footage we co-produced with a small but brilliant band of computer geniuses serving as our subcontractors. It was imperative for *them* to stay on *their* production schedule at every point along the process so that we could stay on *our* production schedule and deliver the film to the clients on time.

At the beginning of production as co-producer of the film, I asked our subcontractors (the computer geniuses) to make out a very detailed production schedule that would document precisely how they would achieve their production deadlines for each scene in the film.

They came back to me with a very impressive-looking PERT chart, extremely dense with data. (A PERT chart is a kind of production schedule that has labeled boxes with scheduling details, all connected together with one massive spider web of sequential dependency lines.) It nearly covered an entire wall in my office.

Even though their schedule looked impressive, God was about to save us from disaster by showing us something we couldn't see. We had been fervently praying for the success of this project every day for months during pre-production, and that could have been the reason why my spiritual antennae was more sensitive than usual to pick up what God wanted to tell me.

[I believe God talks to all of us all the time—so my reference to God telling me something simply puts me in the same league with everyone else. The key, however, is for all of us to actively keep listening for what He is saying . . . really, as a way of life.]

A few days after the subcontractors handed us the PERT chart, I was studying it on my office wall. Suddenly, out of the blue, God gave me a download, a word of knowledge: information from the mind of God suddenly zapped into my own mind. As a result, I saw something that I wasn't actually seeing with my eyes. (It was sort of like seeing my friend Gwennie with my eyes shut!)

This download came to me in just a flash by the Holy Spirit, but here it is, unpacked and expressed in words:

"Since different people are working different amounts of time on different jobs over the course of the project with simultaneously overlapping duties and processes, the subcontractor's impressive PERT chart is doing nothing to prove that there are not, in fact, *resource conflicts*. The problem of people being spread too thin is not visible in this schedule. It is neither confirmed or denied. However, Bob . . . there ARE resource conflicts here! Run it through your own computer!"

I had no reason to doubt our tech team; they were among the most cutting-edge talents in the industry. So I was totally stunned by this sudden warning. But I trusted the Holy Spirit more.

In response, I began hastily re-entering the massive information from their PERT chart (tasks, resources, scenes, time, etc.) into my own computer's scheduling program over the next two days.

After I got their schedule data into my computer, I ran a resource conflict check (which they never did).

Shazam! My computer confirmed what God had been telling me: *they had overbooked manpower by as much as three times in some cases!* But this was not visible at all on their wonderful-looking chart.

What the subcontractors gave us was essentially a worthless schedule (though they didn't intend for it to be). Therefore, it was going to be impossible for us to meet our December 3 deadline with our client because it would be impossible for *them* to meet *their* deadlines first. The existing resources were not sufficient. For example, some technical directors, who were required to supervise entire movie scenes, had been scheduled for as much as thirty-six hours each day (an obvious impossibility) though you wouldn't have known that by looking at their massive schedule.

We called an emergency meeting. We presented our subcontractors with our own schedule that proved our case. They couldn't deny the math: more resources had to be acquired—on their dime—in order to meet the project deadline.

Bound by contract, they had to face the facts— they were compelled from a legal standpoint to provide more people and more equipment in order to fulfill the contract they had initially signed with us.

This discovery, which we made totally from God's supernatural intervention, was made early in the production. This saved our film company from disaster. If God had not shown us these resource conflicts early on, we would have discovered, far too late, that we were functioning with insufficient resources.

If that crisis had played out, our reputations could have been ruined, and we likely would have had to sell our homes or take some other drastic measure to pay for the loss to both our U.S. and Japanese clients.

Even though we had to conduct several meetings that were intense and confrontational (sometimes mandatory in business), we didn't hate these people at all. We didn't abuse them. Although we had to be firm and direct, we administered the meetings with respect.

Ultimately, when you're praying for people, you just tend to love them, even if you have to (proverbially) grab their faces, stare into their eyes, and say sternly, "Fix this problem!"

We had never told them we were believers in Jesus. We weren't ashamed of our faith. It's just that there was too much pressure from the get-go, too much business to cover, and the people we were dealing with were a very unique breed. Most of them came from a very "edgy" realm. (Visualize this mixture: punk-rock, math geeks, gothic, counter-culture, MIT grads, young Einsteins.) Well, with such people, we felt that sharing our faith would have required a significant amount of ramp-up time and cultivation of relationship before our testimony would be received.

However, Jesus can make Himself known in any atmosphere, especially when lots of prayers are being offered up from the sidelines. He can make His fragrance exude sweetly, even in the kind of high-pressure production environment I just described. I'm not sure how He does it, but here's an illustration . . .

We made the project deadline with just four days to spare after a year-and-a-half schedule. That shows just how close it was and how urgently we had needed God's revelation, early on, about resource conflicts so the project didn't drag on another three to four months.

As the project came to a happy conclusion, one of the key animation producers working for us took me into a side room and shut the door. I had no idea what to expect. She is a sophisticated woman, a sharp producer out of New York, hired to help get the animation done on time. In fact, she was one of several people we had to confront, months prior, about resource conflicts when the logistical crisis hit the fan.

She looked me in the eye and said, "Okay, Bob. So, tell me about this Jesus."

My mouth fell open. I was stunned. I couldn't figure out how she even knew. So I asked, "How did you even know . . . I mean what . . . "

She nodded, "We knew. Trust me, we knew. Tell me about Him."

So, still amazed, I explained the whole plan of salvation and how much Jesus loves her. I explained that this salvation is not a religious issue, but more of an accounting issue. We're born into this world spiritually dead. Each of us has a huge debt before God which none of us can ever pay because we are born in sin, and the penalty of sin is spiritual death—separation from God forever. So God faced a dilemma: how can He act on His perfect love by saving us from our hopeless state, yet remain true to His absolute laws of right and wrong, whereby sin must be punished by death? The Cross, of course, is where God's justice and mercy meet.

The producer drank in every word. She was transfixed. After I finished, she did not fall down on her knees yelling, "Hallelujah, brother! I see the light!" (I would have questioned such odd behavior if she had!) Instead, she thanked me and said she would really need to ponder all that I had given her.

And for that, I was grateful, though still amazed at how God had begun a hunger in her to know Him, even in the middle of the wild and chaotic pressures of film production.

God wants to work miracles everywhere: in the workplace, on vacation, at the store . . . and my hope is that we will never be tempted to refuse Him permission to do miracles in our churches as well.

"We pull on you, God!"